THE CAREER CONNECTION FOR COLLEGE EDUCATION

A Guide to College Majors and Related Career Opportunities

Second Edition

Fred A. Rowe, Ed. D.

Second Edition

The Career Connection for College Education—A Guide to College Majors and Related Career Opportunities

©1994, JIST Works, Inc.

JIST Works, Inc.
720 North Park Avenue
Indianapolis, IN 46202–3431
1-317-264-3720 • Fax: 1-317-264-3709

The Career Connection for Technical Education
Another book by Dr. Rowe that uses a format similar to this book
but is for those considering technical majors. Price: $14.95
ISBN: 1-56370-143-X

Other Titles: JIST publishes a variety of career reference books on job
seeking and career information.
Order Information: See the last page of this book for an order form or contact us
for additional information. Qualified schools and institutions may request our
catalog of more than 500 career-related books, videos, and software.
Errors and omissions: We have been careful to provide accurate information throughout this
book, but it is possible that errors have been inadvertently introduced. Please consider this
in making any career plans or other important decisions. Trust your own judgment above all
else and in all things.

Library of Congress Cataloging-In-Publications Data

Rowe, Fred A.
    The career connection for college education : a guide to college
majors and related career opportunities / Fred A. Rowe. — 2d ed.
      p.   cm.
    Rev. ed. of: The career connection. Rev. ed. c1991.
    Includes indexes.
    ISBN 1-56370-142-1
    1. Vocational guidance—United States—Handbooks, manuals, etc.
2. Occupations—United States—Handbooks, manuals, etc.
3. Vocational qualifications—United States—Handbooks, manuals,
etc.   4. College majors—United Staes—Handbooks, manuals, etc.
5. College graduates—Employment—United States—Handbooks, manuals,
etc.   I. Rowe, Fred A. Career connection. II. Title.
HF5382.5.U5R68 1994
331.7'02—dc20   94-15662
                                                    CIP

ISBN: 1-56370-142-1

Table of Contents

The Reasons This Book Is Important to You   v

Target Groups Helped by This Book   vi

How to Use This Book   viii

Getting to Know Yourself and the World of Work and Education   1

Your Occupational Personality Style 3
Courses 8
Your Interest Areas 12
Working with Data, People, or Things 20

100 College Majors and Their Career Opportunities   25

This section describes more than 100 college majors including: Description • Emphases Within Each Major • Typical College Courses • Related High School Courses • Related Careers with Beginning Salaries and Outlook • Related Occupational Personality Styles • Data, People, Things Level of Functioning • GOE Work Groups

Accounting 26
Advertising 28
Aerospace and aeronautical
     engineering 30
African studies 32
Agricultural economics 34
Agronomy 36
American studies 38
Animal science 40
Anthropology 42
Architecture 44
Art..46
Asian studies 48
Botony..50
Business education 52
Business management 54
Canadian studies 56
Chemical engineering 58
Chemistry 60

Chinese 62
Civil engineering...........................64
Classical languages.......................66
Clothing and textiles 68
Commercial art, design
     and photography 70
Communications 72
Community health education 74
Computer science 76
Dance and physical education 78
Dentistry 80
Design and illustration 82
Design engineering technology.....84
Dietetics 86
Drafting..88
Early childhood education 90
Economics 92
Educational psychology 94
Electrical engineering 96

Electronics engineering technology ... 98
Elementary education ... 100
English ... 102
Environmental health ... 104
European studies ... 106
Family resource management ... 108
Finance and banking ... 110
Food science ... 112
Forestry ... 114
French ... 116
Genealogy ... 118
Geography ... 120
Geology ... 122
Geophysics ... 124
German ... 126
Health administration ... 128
Health science ... 130
History ... 132
Home economics education ... 134
Horticulture ... 136
Hotel management ... 138
Industrial administration ... 140
Industrial education ... 142
Information management ... 144
Insurance ... 146
Japanese ... 148
Journalism ... 150
Landscape architecture ... 152
Latin American studies ... 154
Law ... 156
Library science ... 158
Linguistics ... 160
Manufacturing engineering technology ... 162
Marketing and retailing ... 164
Mathematics ... 166
Mechanical engineering ... 168

Medical technology ... 170
Medicine ... 172
Metallurgical engineering ... 174
Microbiology ... 176
Mining and geological engineering ... 178
Music ... 180
Near Eastern studies ... 182
Nursing ... 184
Occupational health and safety ... 186
Occupational therapy ... 188
Oceanography ... 190
Optometry ... 192
Pharmacy ... 194
Philosophy ... 196
Physical education ... 198
Physical therapy ... 200
Physics and astronomy ... 202
Political science ... 204
Portuguese ... 206
Psychology ... 208
Public administration ... 210
Public relations ... 212
Range management ... 214
Recreation management ... 216
Russian ... 218
Secondary education ... 220
Social work ... 222
Sociology ... 224
Spanish ... 226
Special education ... 228
Speech pathology and audiology ... 230
Statistics ... 232
Theater and cinematic arts ... 234
Veterinary medicine ... 236
Wildlife management ... 238
Youth leadership ... 240
Zoology ... 242

Auxiliary Information   244

The Relationship Between Education and Careers ... 245
Alternatives for Post-High School Education ... 245
Ideas on Admissions ... 247
The Anatomy of a Job ... 251

Indexes   254

Index of Majors ... 255
Index of Careers ... 257

The Reasons This Book Is Important to You

The fact that you are reading this book indicates your interest in the possibility of further education. That is a big decision. It affects not only what you will be doing in the short term but also the circumstances surrounding your work and your lifestyle. Education affects careers, and careers have an impact on our lives. Families, geography, self-worth, and financial resources are all integrated so completely with our work.

For most people, the period between ages 16 and 25 is a peak time for decision making. This is when they determine educational goals, select a technical school or university, find a major, decide on a career, and begin a career path. With the increasing demands of the labor market, more and more adults also find the need to make important career, education, and training decisions. These decisions are important and require a heavy investment in both time and energy.

Because selecting a career is so vital, nearly everyone needs help with it. It is true that most students will receive career information of one kind or another: some will receive it from an important acquaintance, others will find it by chance, and many will receive structured career counseling.

Career decision making is not, as some may believe, a linear process. One usually does not first pick a college, next choose an appropriate major, and then select a career. Nor does one select a career, next choose an appropriate major, and then pick a college offering that curriculum. Many times, students will hop into the middle of the process and select a major first; or more precisely, they will enroll in courses and then see if they are happy and successful.

Selecting a major and narrowing the possibilities for a career can be exciting. You are the most important person in your life. The quality of your happiness, self-fulfillment, and service is dramatically influenced by how well you plan.

Although career decision making is a complex process, it becomes a lot easier if you

1. know who you are, what you can do, and what you want out of life;
2. have a pool of career and educational information; and
3. talk with knowledgeable people who can help you harmonize who you are with the educational and career alternatives that are acceptable and accessible to you.

Target Groups Helped by This Book

The Career Connection for College Education provides a variety of information arranged in a simple-to-use format that is useful to many types of individuals.

Students Both high school and college students need information about themselves and educational or career alternatives. The times when this book can be of most help are:
- At registration times when you have to select those courses that may be most helpful in preparing you for college, or to actually enroll in college
- When you have general questions about how much education you want after high school
- As you have some questions about a few careers that seem high on your list and you want to know what educational majors these are related to
- When you work with counselors, friends, and parents in registering for your first semester at college
- As you try to narrow down the possibilities of a college major
- At those times when you are wondering what your personality and interests are and how they relate to careers

Counselors This book is a particularly valuable resource for both high school and college counselors. Its advantage over encyclopedia-type reference books are (a) its ease of reading, (b) the broad variety of information, and (c) the frequency with which students will use it. Here are some times when this book has proven to be most useful.
- At registration
- For classes in career education as a textbook—its ability to help students understand themselves, then use that self-awareness to contemplate educational and career opportunities is effective
- When helping students plan for college, college admissions, and first enrollment
- In small group experiences with students
- With parents and students in small groups as they plan for their high school registrations and college day activities
- In college career classes
- In school career centers, as a valuable resource with other college catalogs

Parents Parental involvement in their children's education is continually sought by educators and its value is unsurpassed. Simply put, families have the greatest impact on youth decisions for careers. Here are some ways you can use this book.

- To show students the relationship between careers and education
- At critical points in their high school and college careers, such as when entering high school and in the transition from high school to college
- When attempting to help your children understand themselves better in areas of personality types that relate to careers, how their school courses can be a barometer for college majors, and how their interests relate to college and careers
- When providing information about education and careers that is hard to pick out of large encyclopedias
- As your children become lost, bored, or uneasy about the meaning of their educational experiences
- To help them look at a broader expanse of career and educational opportunities that may not have been available to you as a parent

Teachers While most classes are not thought of as career preparatory classes, their meaning can be increased to students by relating what is being learned in class to further educational and occupational realms. Here are a few ideas.

- A quick reference to careers and majors related to your classes
- A way to self-exploration
- As a guide to those students who seem lost or uncertain
- To broaden the vision of students who have gender issues related to accessible career opportunities

Career Changers and Displaced Workers This is a critical time in one's life—a time when thoughts turn to retraining. For displaced homemakers trying to be both parents, breadwinner, and student, ideas for short-term training seem applicable. For displaced workers, the emphasis to catch up on current methods, ideas, and knowledge is imperative. Here are a few ideas that can help you use this book.

- To identify who you are—this is a critical issue when disappointment has bludgeoned your self-esteem
- To see what is available on the current market and what the salaries and outlooks are
- When re-evaluating your original desires for the amount of education you wanted
- To compare the length of time and commitment needed to major in certain areas that seem acceptable to you
- To compare your personality style, interests, and the skills you already possess with related jobs and educational areas

How to Use This Book

The book has been designed to be flexible by providing several ways to approach the career exploration process. You can use the Table of Contents to quickly identify a college major, then turn to that section in the book for more detailed information. You can also look up a specific job title in the Career Index and find its related educational requirements. Another very effective way is to identify what you are like in relation to careers and college majors. *The Career Connection for College Education* is divided into seven major sections.

Part One This is the introductory section on The Reasons This Book Is Important to You.

Part Two There are several groups of people that can benefit from *The Career Connection for College Education*. They are identified with various ways of utilizing the information within the book.

Part Three The value of important information in the process of career and educational decision making is discussed.

Part Four This section provides you an opportunity to study yourself and see how your personality and interests, along with your inclination to work with information, people, or concrete objects, relate to various college majors and work groups. It includes
1. A description of various occupational personality styles and their relationships to college majors and the *Guide for Occupational Exploration* (GOE) interest area work groups
2. A description of the various GOE work groups and their relationship to the college majors
3. Types of school courses or subjects and their relationship to the various college majors and GOE work groups
4. What functions are considered in working with data, people, or things and the college majors and GOE work groups that have "high" requirements in each of those three categories

Part Five This section describes more than 100 college majors, including:
1. A general description of each college major and the type of career-related work it leads to

2. Various job titles, outlook for future openings, and starting salaries related to each major
3. A code number for each occupation that cross-references the reader to the *Dictionary of Occupational Titles*, a major career information source published by the U.S. Department of Labor
4. The types of courses typically required in each area of study
5. High school courses that best prepare for the area of study or that indicate an ability to succeed in that area
6. The occupational personality styles that are best for the major
7. Whether the major requires tasks that are high, medium, or low in the areas of working with data, people, or things
8. The general interest areas of the *Guide for Occupational Exploration* that relate to the specific major

Part Six This part includes ideas concerning
1. The relationship between levels of education and careers
2. The different types of educational opportunities after high school
3. Ideas on admissions
4. The anatomy of a job

Part Seven For easier access to the various college majors and their related careers, two indexes are provided. The first is an alphabetical listing of the majors and their corresponding page numbers. The second index provides an alphabetical listing of nearly 1,000 careers and their corresponding page numbers. It will be noted that many careers can emerge from more than one college major.

This variety of information is provided in a simple-to-use format that should be useful for most users. The information is general in nature and can't replace the careful review of a school's catalog of course offerings and requirements. Many schools will have specific requirements that may differ from those presented here and the names of their major areas of study may also differ. But the information contained here is helpful in identifying areas of interest that are worthy of more consideration.

Information that resulted in the projection of beginning salaries was derived from (a) 16 specifically selected college and university placement offices, (b) national professional organizations, (c) regional manpower studies printed by the information services of Job Service, and (d) national publications including "Federal Civilian Workforce Statistics: Occupations of Federal White-Collar and Blue-Collar Workers," printed by the U.S. Office of Personnel Management; and "Comparison of Annual Salaries in Private Industry with Salary Rates of Federal Employees," and the "General Schedule: National Survey of Professional, Administrative, Technical, and Clerical Pay," printed by the U.S. Department of Labor, Bureau of Labor Statistics.

This government publication is often found in the offices of most counselors or in career centers and libraries. It provides descriptions of over 12,000 jobs and is an important reference for you to know about.

If an occupation is included in this publication, it has a reference number which is actually a code. By looking up the title, you can read a brief description about the job and environment along with some ideas of tasks used on the job.

The sample number is broken down into a working code below:

SAMPLE

005.	061	–	014
Occupational Group	Worker Functions		Alphabetical Order of Titles

OCCUPATIONAL GROUP

The first three digits classify specific occupational groups. The first digit represents nine cluster occupations, including:

0/1	Professional, Technical, and Managerial	5	Processing
2	Clerical and Sales	6	Machine Trades
3	Service	7	Benchwork
4	Agricultural, Fishing, and Forestry	8	Structural Work
		9	Miscellaneous

Degrees associated with college majors are found mostly in the 0/1 and 2 occupational group. The second two digits of the occupational code are categorized into 82 specific divisions such as engineering, education, music, etc.

WORKER FUNCTIONS

The second set of three digits identifies the types of tasks most often associated or used in the specific occupation. When working, according to this government publication, we perform specific tasks centered around DATA, PEOPLE, or THINGS. A particular occupation may emphasize each of these three categories with different intensities. The D.O.T. simply lists the major types of tasks associated with each of the three categories.

4th Digit = **Data**	5th Digit = **People**	6th Digit = **Things**
0 Synthesizing	0 Mentoring	0 Setting Up
1 Coordinating	1 Negotiating	1 Precision Working
2 Analyzing	2 Instructing	2 Operating-Controlling
3 Compiling	3 Supervising	3 Driving-Operating
4 Computing	4 Diverting	4 Manipulating
5 Copying	5 Persuading	5 Tending
6 Comparing	6 Speaking-Signaling	6 Feeding—Offbearing
	7 Serving	7 Handling
	8 Taking Instructions—Helping	

ALPHABETICAL ORDER OF TITLES

The last three digits are merely the general listing of occupations within the first six digits.

EXAMPLE

Occupation: Civil Engineering

D.O.T. Number: 005.061-014

0	Professional, Technical, and Management
00	Engineering
005	Civil Engineering
0	Synthesizing data
6	Speaking-Signaling with people
1	Precision working with things
014	Alphabetical listing of Civil Engineering

Getting to Know Yourself and the World of Work and Education

When we purchase a packaged article, such as a bookcase, from a store and take it home, we expect that it contains a set of instructions on how to assemble the article. As we contemplate our careers and the educational possibilities in which we might become involved, it often seems that there is no packaged program nor are there any specific directions on how to put the various parts together.

Careers impact our lives. Families, geography, self-worth, and lifestyle are all integrated completely with our work. Let's look at families to illustrate this point. Research has shown that families who have traditions in which parents, siblings, aunts, and uncles have careers in semi-skilled work, for example, will generate children who gravitate toward this type of career in their life. The professional family tradition will generate children who are more interested in that area of occupational involvement than others. Another example of how careers influence us is when a change in a parent's career affects where the family will live, with whom they will associate, the financial resources available, and school involvement.

As we look into our personal possibilities for future career connections, we screen everything through two important filters. First is the filter of self-awareness. Second is the filter of our knowledge about the world of education and work. Decision making is the process of integrating what we know of ourselves with what we know about the world, then identifying those careers or college majors that are both acceptable and accessible to us.

In this section, you will be able to see yourself in light of

1. Your occupational personality style
2. School courses you like and dislike
3. Your interest areas
4. Functions you like related to working with data, people, or things

For each of the four topics, use the following chart to identify the areas that you like. Since each of the topics show how it is related to college majors and work areas, going through the exercises will show a pattern. Finding those majors and career areas that continually "show up" for you can direct you toward more information in the rest of this book.

Look over the following **Personal Summary Chart**, then proceed through the rest of Part Four. If it is easier, make a copy of the **Personal Summary Chart** to work from.

PERSONAL SUMMARY CHART

Name _____ Date _____

TOPICS

Write in the answers that most closely describe you.

COLLEGE MAJORS

Below, list the college majors that relate to your answers in the topic section.

GOE WORK GROUPS

Below, list the GOE work groups that relate to your answers in the topic section.

My Occupational Personality Styles

1 _____ _____ _____

2 _____ _____ _____

3 _____ _____ _____

School Subject Areas That I Like Most

1 _____ _____ _____

2 _____ _____ _____

3 _____ _____ _____

My Highest Interest Work Groups

1 _____ _____ _____

2 _____ _____ _____

3 _____ _____ _____

I am "High," "Medium," or "Low" in being good at and enjoying working with data, people, or things

____ Data

____ People

____ Things

The Career Connection for College Education

For decades people have been trying to match people to jobs. A particularly helpful development occurred when the idea of personality types emerged. The notion is that specific personality types can be identified in people. There are also careers that harmonize with particular personality types. When a person is successful in becoming aware of what they are like and finding a college major and subsequent careers that parallel their inclinations, several very positive consequences occur. Some of them are:

1. Self-confidence
2. Self-worth
3. Greater contributions to _____
4. Ability to handle discouragement and obstacles
5. Good relationships with peers and supervisors
6. Feelings of self-fulfillment
7. Fewer illnesses and lower absenteeism
8. General feeling of control over life
9. Less feeling of stress and strain
10. General aura of joy and fascination with life

Seven occupational personality styles can be identified. We all have each of these styles in us; however, we typically peak out in two or three in particular.

Their descriptions are as follows:

Artistic Enjoys expressing oneself; unstructured; not particularly sociable except to selected people; enthusiastic about one's activities

Detail-oriented Persistent; enjoys routine and structure; slow to change; intense about beliefs; looks to authority; hard-working

Influencing Sees self as persuasive; good communicator; plans and organizes; entrepreneurial; likes to risk; not particularly academic; action-oriented

Scientific Deals in abstractions and symbols; sometimes appears cynical; curious; analytical; doesn't need a lot of friends; careful in one's work

Serving Persuasively helps others; not necessarily gregarious; altruistic; likes to present and teach; introspective; sensitive to others

Social Enjoys being around people; sees self as an effective communicator; solves problems by asking what others think; interaction is more important than task accomplishment

Technical Solves problems by working with concrete objects; genuine; frank; athletically oriented; not too social with a lot of people; slow to change

When one identifies which two or three styles most closely describe him or her, it is a big step toward locating jobs acceptable to preferred lifestyle and personal inclinations.

OCCUPATIONAL PERSONALITY STYLES AND THEIR RELATIONSHIP TO COLLEGE MAJORS AND CAREERS

Style	College Majors	GOE Work Groups
Artistic		
	Advertising	Craft Arts 01.06
	Architecture	Performing Arts: Dance 01.05
	Art	Performing Arts: Drama 01.03
	Commercial Art, Design,	Performing Arts: Music 01.04
	and Photography	Visual Arts 01.02
	Dance and Physical Education	
	Design and Illustration	
	Landscape Architecture	
	Music	
	Theater and Cinematic Arts	
Detail-oriented		
	Accounting	Administrative Detail 07.01
	Agricultural Economics	Educational and Library
	Business Education	Services 11.02
	Computer Science	Finance 11.06
	Drafting	Financial Detail 07.03
	Finance and Banking	Mathematical Detail 07.02
	Genealogy	Mathematics and Statistics
	Information Management	11.01
	Library Science	
	Manufacturing Technology	
	Pharmacy	
	Statistics	
Influencing		
	Business Management	Business Administration 11.05
	Communications	Business Management 11.11
	Family Resource Management	Communications 11.08

Style	College Majors	GOE Work Groups

Influencing

Health Administration	Customer Services 09.04
Hotel Management	General Sales 08.02
Industrial Management	Hospitality Services 09.01
Insurance	Law 11.04
Journalism	Literary Arts 01.01
Law	Promotion 11.09
Marketing and Retailing	
Political Science	
Public Administration	
Public Relations	
Recreation Management	
Wildlife Management	
Youth Leadership	

Scientific

Aerospace and Aeronautical Engineering	Engineering 05.01
African Studies	Engineering Technology 05.03
Agricultural Economics	Laboratory Technology 02.04
Agronomy	Life Sciences 02.02
American Studies	Mathematics and Statistics 11.01
Animal Science	Medical Sciences 02.03
Anthropology	Nursing, Therapy, and Specialized Teaching Services 10.02
Asian Studies	
Botany	
Canadian Studies	Physical Sciences 02.01
Chemical Engineering	Social Research 11.03
Chemistry	Social Services 10.01
Civil Engineering	
Classical Languages	
Computer Science	
Dentistry	
Dietetics	
Economics	
Educational Psychology	
Electrical Engineering	
English	
Environmental Health	
European Studies	
Food Science	
Forestry	
Geography	

Style	College Majors	GOE Work Groups

Scientific

Geology
Geophysics
Health Science
History
Latin American Studies
Linguistics
Mathematics
Mechanical Engineering
Medical Technology
Medicine
Metallurgical Engineering
Microbiology
Mining and Geological Engineering
Near Eastern Studies
Nursing
Oceanography
Philosophy
Physics and Astronomy
Psychology
Social Work
Sociology
Speech Pathology and Audiology
Veterinary Medicine
Zoology

Serving

Business Education
Chinese
Community Health Education
Dentistry
Early Childhood Education
Educational Psychology
Elementary Education
French
German
Home Economics Education
Industrial Education
Japanese
Library Science
Medicine
Occupational Health and Safety
Occupational Therapy

Child and Adult Care 10.03
Educational and Library
   Services 11.02
Hospitality Services 09.01
Nursing, Therapy, and
   Specialized Teaching
   Services 10.02
Services Administration
   11.07
Social Services 10.01

The Career Connection for College Education

Style	College Majors	GOE Work Groups

Serving

Optometry
Physical Education
Physical Therapy
Portuguese
Russian
Secondary Education
Social Work
Spanish
Special Education
Speech Pathology and Audiology
Youth Leadership

Social

Business Education
Business Management
Chinese
Community Health Education
Early Childhood Education
Educational Psychology
Elementary Education
European Studies
Family Resource Management
French
German
Health Administration
Home Economics Education
Insurance
Japanese
Latin American Studies
Law
Near Eastern Studies
Nursing
Portuguese
Psychology
Recreation Management
Russian
Secondary Education
Social Work
Sociology
Spanish
Special Education
Youth Leadership

Business Administration 11.05
Business Management 11.11
Child and Adult Care 10.03
Customer Services 09.04
General Sales 08.02
Hospitality Services 09.01
Nursing, Therapy, and
   Specialized Teaching
   Services 10.02
Services Administration
   11.07
Social Services 10.01

Technical

	College Majors	GOE Work Groups
	Aerospace and Aeronautical Engineering	Engineering 05.01
	Civil Engineering	Engineering Technology 05.03
	Dance and Physical Education	Quality Control 05.07
	Dentistry	Sports 12.01
	Drafting	Systems Operation 05.06
	Electronics Engineering Technology	
	Forestry	
	Landscape Architecture	
	Manufacturing Technology	
	Medical Technology	
	Metallurgical Engineering	
	Mining and Geological Engineering	
	Optometry	
	Physical Education	
	Physical Therapy	
	Range Management	
	Speech Pathology and Audiology	
	Veterinary Medicine	

COURSES

How well people like their high school courses predict fairly well how they will enjoy similar courses in college. Most people also earn their highest grades in college courses similar to the high school courses in which they did well. We tend to gravitate to those majors that are compatible and will direct us toward desirable career opportunities.

It will help to identify the courses one enjoyed and look at related college majors and career areas that may be relevant.

SCHOOL SUBJECTS AND THEIR RELATIONSHIP TO COLLEGE MAJORS AND CAREERS

Course Category	College Majors	GOE Work Groups

Business

	College Majors	GOE Work Groups
	Accounting	Administrative Detail 07.01
	Advertising	Business Administration 11.05
	Business Education	Business Management 11.11
	Business Management	Sales Technology 08.01
	Economics	
	Family Resource Management	
	Finance and Banking	
	Health Administration	
	Hotel Management	
	Industrial Administration	
	Information Management	
	Insurance	
	Marketing and Retailing	
	Occupational Therapy	
	Public Administration	
	Public Relations	

Fine Arts

	College Majors	GOE Work Groups
	Architecture	Craft Arts 01.06
	Art	Performing Arts 01.05
	Commercial Art, Design, and Photography	Performing Arts 01.03
		Performing Arts 01.04
	Dance and Physical Education	Visual Arts 01.02
	Design and Illustration	
	Music	
	Theater and Cinematic Arts	

Language Arts

	College Majors	GOE Work Groups
	Chinese	Communications 11.08
	Classical Languages	Literary Arts 01.01
	Communications	
	English	
	French	
	German	
	Information Management	
	Japanese	
	Journalism	
	Law	
	Library Science	
	Linguistics	
	Portuguese	

Language Arts
Russian
Spanish

Mathematics
Aerospace and Aeronautical
  Engineering
Agricultural Economics
Architecture
Chemical Engineering
Chemistry
Civil Engineering
Computer Science
Design Engineering Technology
Economics
Electrical Engineering
Electronics Engineering Technology
Geophysics
Mathematics
Mechanical Engineering
Metallurgical Engineering
Mining and Geological Engineering
Physics and Astronomy
Statistics

Engineering 05.01
Engineering Technology 05.03
Mathematics and Statistics
  11.01
Physical Sciences 02.01
Social Research 11.03
Systems Operation 05.06

Natural and Physical Sciences
Botany
Chemistry
Dentistry
Dietetics
Forestry
Geology
Geophysics
Medical Technology
Medicine
Microbiology
Nursing
Optometry
Pharmacy
Physical Therapy
Speech Pathology and Audiology
Veterinary Medicine
Wildlife Management
Zoology

Laboratory Technology 02.04
Life Sciences 02.02
Medical Sciences 02.03
Nursing, Therapy, and
  Specialized Teaching
  Services 10.02
Physical Sciences 02.01

Course Category	College Majors	GOE Work Groups

Physical Education

Community Health Education	Hospitality Services 09.01
Dance and Physical Education	Performing Arts: Dance 01.05
Dietetics	Services Administration 11.07
Environmental Health	Sports 12.01
Health Administration	
Health Science	
Physical Education	
Recreation Management	
Youth Leadership	

Social Science

African Studies	Educational and Library
Agricultural Economics	Services 11.02
American Studies	Social Research 11.03
Anthropology	Social Services 10.01
Asian Studies	
Canadian Studies	
Classical Languages	
Early Childhood Education	
Economics	
Educational Psychology	
Elementary Education	
European Studies	
Genealogy	
Geography	
History	
Latin American Studies	
Law	
Near Eastern Studies	
Occupational Therapy	
Philosophy	
Political Science	
Psychology	
Secondary Education	
Social Work	
Sociology	
Special Education	
Youth Leadership	

Vocational

Agricultural Economics	Clerical Machine Operation
Agronomy	07.06
Animal Science	Clerical Handling 07.07
Clothing and Textiles	Contracts and Claims 11.12
Dietetics	Crafts 05.10

Course Category	College Majors	GOE Work Groups

Vocational

	College Majors	GOE Work Groups
	Early Childhood Education	Life Sciences 02.02
	Food Science	Managerial Work: Plants and Animals 03.01
	Home Economics Education	Quality Control 05.07
	Horticulture	Regulations Enforcement 11.10
	Range Management	Safety and Law Enforcement 04.01

YOUR INTEREST AREAS

Different people like different things. Likes are based in part on the experiences you have had and how well you enjoyed them. There may also be areas of interest which you know little about or with which you have had little experience.

As one explores educational majors and various occupations, it is important to look at your interests and compare them with various occupations or categories of occupations. A government task force has identified 12 categories of interests. Each category is further divided into work groups. In total there are 66 work groups. Each work group is described and typical jobs are listed. The various interest areas and work groups are coded and included in *The Complete Guide for Occupational Exploration* (CGOE).

Forty work groups are closely associated with majors found on typical college and university campuses. They are described below.

ARTISTIC 01 *Creatively expressing your ideas or feelings*

Literary Arts 01.01
Working with written expression such as editing, creative writing, critiquing, or publishing
Visual Arts 01.02
Creating original art through studio work, commercial art instructing, and directing
Performing Arts: Drama 01.03
Working in dramatic productions in the areas of performance, composing, arranging, instructing, and directing
Performing Arts: Music 01.04
Participating in the musical arena by vocal performance, composing, arranging, instructing, and directing

Performing Arts: Dance 01.05
Contributing to dance through performance, instruction, and chore-ography
Craft Arts 01.06
Using artistic methods to make, decorate, or repair products

SCIENTIFIC 02 *Analyzing information gathered through research to solve problems in the natural world*

Physical Sciences 02.01
Applying technology and research in the study of non-living things
Life Sciences 02.02
Understanding living things through animal specialization, plant specialization, and food research
Medical Sciences 02.03
Relieving human or animal distress by means of dentistry, veteri-nary medicine, health specialties, services, and surgery
Laboratory Technology 02.04
Assisting physical scientists or life scientists by conducting and re-cording research for them

PLANTS AND ANIMALS 03 *Studying plants and animals in their natural environment*

Managerial Work: Plants and Animals 03.01
Managing businesses that deal with plants and animals such as farm-ing, specialty breeding, specialty cropping, forestry, and logging

PROTECTIVE 04 *Guarding the lives and property of others*

Safety and Law Enforcement 04.01
Compelling others to obey the laws through positions in manage-ment and investigation

MECHANICAL 05 *Using hands and tools to create or repair objects*

Engineering 05.01
Generating and carrying out ideas for construction projects in re-search, environmental protection, systems design, sales engineering testing, quality control, design, general engineering, work planning and utilization
Engineering Technology 05.03
Gathering information for others as a surveyor, drafter, expediter and coordinator in the areas of petroleum, electrical-electronic in-dustry, mechanics, environmental control, packaging, and storing

Systems Operation 05.06
Servicing equipment that is part of a larger system as in electricity generation and transmission, stationary engineering, oil, gas and water distribution, and processing

Quality Control 05.07
Checking products for compliance with set standards in the mechanical, electrical, environmental, petroleum, structural, logging, and lumber fields

Crafts 05.10
Using hands and hand tools with skill to make, process, install, and repair materials, products, and structural parts

INDUSTRIAL 06 *Applying skills to perform repetitive, structured tasks*

(None applicable to college majors)

BUSINESS DETAIL 07 *Carrying out specified tasks in an office setting*

Administrative Detail 07.01
Tending to high-level clerical work requiring special skills and knowledge

Mathematical Detail 07.02
Overseeing the mathematical details such as organizing, collecting, computing, and recording numerical information in business and financial transactions

Financial Detail 07.03
Using basic arithmetic where money is paid out or received from the public

Clerical Machine Operation 07.06
Using machines such as computers and keyboard machines to organize data

Clerical Handling 07.07
Carrying out tasks in an office which require little skill, such as filing, sorting, distributing, and general clerical work

SELLING 08 *Presenting goods or services to people and persuading them to purchase*

Sales Technology 08.01
Selling technical products and services and consulting with customers about purchasing and sales

General Sales 08.02
Demonstrating and selling products in many different settings, such as wholesale, retail, real estate, and services

The Career Connection for College Education

ACCOMMODATING 09 *Caring for the needs of others*

(None applicable to college majors)

HUMANITARIAN 10 *Caring for the health needs of others*

Social Services 10.01
> Meeting with groups or individuals to help them understand and
> deal with their problems from a religious or counseling viewpoint

Nursing, Therapy, and Specialized Teaching Services 10.02
> Aiding in improving the physical and emotional health of others as a
> nurse, therapist, or teacher

Child and Adult Care 10.03
> Helping others meet their physical needs through data collection,
> patient care, and general care such as foster care

LEADING-INFLUENCING 11 *Using leadership abilities and other skills to
guide people in thought and action*

Mathematical and Statistics 11.01
> Applying mathematical skills in data processing design and data
> analysis

Educational and Library Services 11.02
> Working in an educational setting as a librarian or as a teacher of
> subjects such as home economics and vocational studies

Social Research 11.03
> Conducting psychological, sociological, historical, occupational, and
> economic research on individuals or groups

Law 11.04
> Attending to the legal matters of others through legal practice, docu-
> ment preparation, justice administration, and conciliation

Business Administration 11.05
> Making decisions and supervising others in government and
> nongovernment establishments

Finance 11.06
> Applying mathematical skills to handle the financial aspects of a bus-
> iness, such as accounting, auditing, records, brokering, and budget

Services Administration 11.07
> Overseeing social, health, safety, education, and recreation programs
> provided by businesses which provide such services

Communications 11.08
> Working with the media such as editing, writing, broadcasting, trans-
> lating, and interpreting factual information

Promotion 11.09
> Presenting products and services in an appealing manner and rais-
> ing money through sales, fund membership solicitation, and public
> relations

Regulations Enforcement 11.10
   Protecting the rights of individuals through enforcement of rules and policies involving finances, health, safety, immigration, and customs
Business Management 11.11
   Supervising all aspects of a business in such areas as lodging, recreation, amusement, transportation, services, and wholesale–retail
Contracts and Claims 11.12
   Arranging contracts and settling claims with renters and leasers; procurement negotiators such as contractors

PHYSICAL PERFORMING 12 *Performing athletics before an audience*

Sports 12.01
   Using athletic abilities to perform in, coach, and officiate sports events

---

GOE WORK GROUPS AND THEIR RELATIONSHIP TO COLLEGE MAJORS

Interest Area	GOE Work Groups	College Majors
Artistic 01		
	Literary Arts 01.01	Communications English History Journalism Philosophy Theater and Cinematic Arts
	Visual Arts 01.02	Art Commercial Art, Design, and Photography Design and Illustration Design Engineering Technology
	Performing Arts: Drama 01.03	Theater and Cinematic Arts
	Performing Arts: Music 01.04	Music
	Performing Arts: Dance 01.05	Dance and Physical Education
Scientific 02		
	Physical Sciences 02.01	Chemistry Geology Geophysics Mathematics Physics and Astronomy

The Career Connection for College Education

Interest Area	GOE Work Groups	College Majors
Scientific 02	Life Sciences 02.02	Botany Food Sciences Forestry Horticulture Microbiology Zoology
	Medical Sciences 02.03	Dentistry Dietetics Health Administration Health Science Medicine Nursing Pharmacy Veterinary Medicine Zoology
	Laboratory Technology 02.04	Medical Technology
Plants and Animals 03	Managerial Work: Plants and Animals 03.01	Animal Science Forestry Horticulture Landscape Architecture Range Management Wildlife Management
Protective 04	Safety and Law Enforcement 04.01	Occupational Health and Safety
Mechanical 05	Engineering 05.01	Aerospace and Aeronautical Engineering Chemical Engineering Civil Engineering Mechanical Engineering Metallurgical Engineering Mining and Geological Engineering
	Engineering Technology 05.03	Architecture Design and Illustration

Interest Area	GOE Work Groups	College Majors

Mechanical 05

		Design Engineering Technology
		Drafting
		Electronics Engineering Technology
		Manufacturing Technology
	Systems Operation 05.06	Industrial Administration
	Quality Control 05.07	Industrial Administration

Industrial 06

None apply

Business Detail 07

	Administrative Detail 07.01	Business Education
		Business Management Communications
		Finance and Banking
		Health Administration
		Hotel Management
		Information Management
		Marketing and Retailing
		Public Administration
		Public Relations
	Mathematical Detail 07.02	Accounting
		Finance and Banking
		Marketing and Retailing
	Financial Detail 07.03	Finance and Banking
	Clerical Machine Operation 07.06	Information Management
	Clerical Handling 07.07	Business Education
		Information Management

Selling 08

	Sales Technology 08.01	Business Education
		Family Resource Management
		Insurance
		Public Relations

Accommodating 09

None Apply

The Career Connection for College Education

Interest Area	GOE Work Groups	College Majors

Humanitarian 10

Social Services 10.01

Educational Psychology
Occupational Therapy
Optometry
Psychology
Social Work
Sociology

Nursing, Therapy, and
Specialized Teaching
Services 10.02

Educational Psychology
Nursing
Occupational Therapy
Physical Therapy
Special Education
Speech Pathology and
  Audiology

Child and Adult Care 10.03

Early Childhood Education
Elementary Education
Nursing
Social Work

Leading–Influencing 11

Mathematics and Statistics 11.01

Computer Science
Economics
Mathematics
Statistics

Educational and Library
Services 11.02

Community Health Education
Early Childhood Education
Elementary Education
Home Economics Education
Industrial Education
Library Science
Secondary Education
Special Education

Social Research 11.03

Advertising
Economics
Educational Psychology
History
Linguistics
Marketing and Retailing
Political Science
Sociology

Interest Area	GOE Work Groups	College Majors

Leading–Influencing 11

	Law 11.04	Law
	Business Administration 11.05	Business Management Finance and Banking Insurance Marketing and Retailing Public Administration
	Finance 11.06	Family Resource Management Finance and Banking Marketing and Retailing
	Services Administration 11.07	Health Administration Occupational Health and Safety Recreation Management Youth Leadership
	Communications 11.08	Communications English Journalism Public Relations Theater and Cinematic Arts
	Promotion 11.09	Advertising Public Relations
	Regulations Enforcement 11.10	Occupational Health and Safety
	Business Management 11.11	Agricultural Economics Business Management Health Administration Recreation Management
	Contracts and Claims 11.12	Insurance

Physical Performing 12

	Sports 12.01	Physical Education

WORKING WITH DATA, PEOPLE, OR THINGS

We perform different functions when working. These functions have been divided into three categories by the government. They are functions dealing with DATA, PEOPLE, or THINGS.

We all have our individual preferences for the types of functions we enjoy and at which we perceive ourselves as doing well. For example, Jed enjoys working with equipment (THINGS) but doesn't particularly relish the idea of presenting ideas to groups or individuals (PEOPLE). Sherry, on the other hand, likes to teach (PEOPLE) and can work for long periods of time on reports for her students (DATA). Give Steve a computer (DATA) and an assignment to design and build a building (THINGS), and he experiences pure joy.

As you contemplate which careers or majors would appeal to you, consider these three major functions and how you see yourself becoming heavily involved with them. It is beneficial to locate those jobs that are not only high in your particular areas of interests and inclinations but also those that are low in the areas of your least desires.

Below, each category is divided into high (abbreviated H in the career outlooks), medium (M), or low (L) levels and is accompanied by the types of activities relevant to each level.

DATA–High	Synthesizing, Coordinating
DATA–Medium	Analyzing, Compiling
DATA–Low	Computing, Copying, Comparing
PEOPLE–High	Mentoring, Negotiating, Instructing
PEOPLE–Medium	Supervising, Diverting, Persuading
PEOPLE–Low	Speaking, Serving, Taking Instructions
THINGS–High	Setting Up, Precision Work
THINGS–Medium	Operating, Driving, Manipulating
THINGS–Low	Tending, Feeding, Handling

When you look at the DOT codes, the middle three numbers represent the DPT levels. The first digit represents DATA; the second, PEOPLE; and the third; THINGS. The higher the number, the more specialized and complex the level of activities required for the particular job.

DATA — PEOPLE — THINGS AND THEIR RELATIONSHIP TO COLLEGE MAJORS AND CAREERS

Category	College Majors	GOE Work Groups
DATA —High	All college majors are high in DATA.	Administrative Detail 07.01
		Business Administration 11.05
		Business Management 11.11
		Child and Adult Care 10.03
		Clerical Handling 07.07
		Communications 11.08
		Contracts and Claims 11.12

Category	College Majors	GOE Work Groups
DATA **—High**	All college majors are high in DATA.	Craft Arts 01.06
		Crafts 05.10
		Educational and Library Services 11.02
		Engineering 05.01
		Engineering Technology 05.03
		Finance 11.06
		General Sales 08.02
		Laboratory Technology 02.04
		Law 11.04
		Life Sciences 02.02
		Literary Arts 01.01
		Managerial Work: Plants and Animals 03.01
		Mathematical Detail 07.02
		Mathematics and Statistics 11.01
		Medical Sciences 02.03
		Performing Arts: Dance 01.05
		Performing Arts: Drama 01.03
		Performing Arts: Music 01.04
		Physical Sciences 02.01
		Promotion 11.09
		Quality Control 05.07
		Regulations Enforcement 11.10
		Safety and Law Enforcement 04.01
		Sales Technology 08.01
		Services Administration 11.07
		Social Research 11.03
		Social Services 10.01
		Sports 12.01
		Systems Operation 05.06
		Visual Arts 11.02
PEOPLE **—High**	Advertising	Business Administration 11.05
	African Studies	Business Management 11.11
	American Studies	Child and Adult Care 10.03
	Asian Studies	Educational and Library Services 11.02
	Business Management	General Sales 08.02
	Canadian Studies	Law 11.04
	Community Health Education	Managerial Work: Plants and Animals 03.01
	Dance and Physical Education	
	Dentistry	

The Career Connection for College Education

Category	College Majors	GOE Work Groups

PEOPLE —High	Dietetics
	Early Childhood Education
	Educational Psychology
	Elementary Education
	Environmental Education
	European Studies
	Family Resource Management
	Finance and Banking
	Food Science
	Geography
	Health Administration
	Health Science
	History
	Home Economics Education
	Hotel Management
	Industrial Administration
	Latin American Studies
	Marketing and Retailing
	Medicine
	Near Eastern Studies
	Nursing
	Optometry
	Physical Education
	Physical Therapy
	Psychology
	Public Administration
	Recreation Management
	Secondary Education
	Social Work
	Sociology
	Special Education
	Speech Pathology and Audiology
	Theater and Cinematic Arts
		Medical Sciences 02.03
		Nursing, Therapy, and
		  Specialized Teaching
		  Services 10.02
		Performing Arts: Dance
		  01.05
		Performing Arts: Drama
		  01.03
		Sales Technology 08.07
		Services Administration
		  11.07
		Social Services 10.01

THINGS —High	Aerospace and Aeronautical
	  Engineering
	Agronomy
	Architecture
	Art
	Botany
	Chemical Engineering
	Chemistry
		Clerical Machine Operation
		  07.06
		Clerical Handling 07.07
		Craft Arts 01.06
		Crafts 05.10
		Engineering 05.01
		Engineering Technology 05.03
		Laboratory Technology 02.04

Category	College Majors	GOE Work Groups

THINGS
—High
	Civil Engineering
	Clothing and Textiles
	Commercial Art, Design,
	  and Photography
	Dentistry
	Design and Illustration
	Design Engineering Technology
	Drafting
	Electrical Engineering
	Electronics Engineering Technology
	Forestry
	Geology
	Horticulture
	Industrial Education
	Medicine
	Microbiology
	Mining and Geological Engineering
	Nursing
	Occupational Health and Safety
	Occupational Therapy
	Oceanography
	Optometry
	Pharmacy
	Physical Therapy
	Physics and Astronomy
	Veterinary Medicine
		Managerial Work: Plants and
		  Animals 03.01
		Sports 12.01

100 College Majors and Their Career Opportunities

Accounting

Tremendous job opportunities are available to accounting majors in management, public, or government accounting. The management accountant provides information and advice as a member of the management team in the planning and direction of the company's operations. The public accountant offers auditing, tax works, and other financial advice services. The Internal Revenue Service, United States Accounting Office, and local and state government agencies provide employment opportunities in government accounting. Employment opportunities continue to increase throughout the United States and in many foreign countries with CPA firms, governments, and industries.

COURSE REQUIREMENTS

Accounting
Auditing
Business Law
Business Mathematics
Business Policy
Computer Science
Economics

Finance
Marketing
Organizational Behavior
Systems

OPTIONS WITHIN MAJOR

Financial Auditing
Management Accounting

Taxation

RECOMMENDED HIGH SCHOOL COURSES

Business Education
English

Math (3 years)
Science

CAREERS	D.O.T. NUMBER	OUTLOOK	AVERAGE INITIAL SALARY
Bachelor Degrees			
Accountant	160.162-018	Excellent	$22,400
Auditor	160.167-054	Good/Exc.	26,100
Bank Examiner	160.167-054	Fair	21,900
Budget and Forecast Accountant	160.162-022	Excellent	25,700
Controller	160.167-058	Fair	25,800
Cost Accountant	160.162-026	Excellent	23,100
General Accountant	160.162-018	Excellent	25,200
Property Accountant	160.167-022	Good	23,900
Revenue Agent	188.167-074	Good	21,400
Securities Trader	186.117-034	Excellent	29,600
Tax Accountant	160.162-010	Excellent	26,300
Graduate Degrees			
Auditor	160.167-054	Excellent	33,600
Bursar	160.167-042	Good	30,400
Professor	090.227-010	Good	32,900
Tax Specialist	160.167-038	Excellent	30,000

Occupational Personality Style: Detail-oriented

DPT Functions: Data = H   People = L   Things = L

GOE Work Group: Mathematical Detail

Advertising

Advertising exists to sell products and services in the marketplace by communicating with the American consumer, who is the best-served user of goods in the world today. It also performs an institutional function by keeping business such as airlines or banks in the public eye. Advertising reminds consumers about what services are available to them. Employment opportunities may be found in advertising agencies, department stores, media, public relations, and professional and trade associations.

COURSE REQUIREMENTS

Advertising, Copy
Advertising Principles
Advertising Strategy
Art
Journalism
Layout Campaigns
Marketing Principles
Media Design

Media Sales Problems
Persuasion Process
Photojournalism
Pictorial Photography
Production
Promotion Management
Retail

OPTIONS WITHIN MAJOR

Business Administration
Design

Journalism
Marketing

RECOMMENDED HIGH SCHOOL COURSES

Art
English (4 years)
History
Journalism

Literature
Speech
Typing

CAREERS	D.O.T. NUMBER	OUTLOOK	AVERAGE INITIAL SALARY
Bachelor Degrees			
Account Executive	164.167-010	Good	$28,600
Advertising Manager	191.167-010	Good	35,500
Commercial Artist	141.061-022	Fair	20,300
Copy Artist	144.061-022	Fair	17,300
Promotion Manager	163.117-018	Good	23,500
Sales Representative	261.257-030	Excellent	22,800
Graduate Degree			
Art Director	188.117-042	Fair	44,000
Professor	090.227-010	Fair	32,900

Occupational Personality Styles: Influencing, Artistic

DPT Functions: Data = H   People = L   Things = M

GOE Work Groups: Business Administration, Promotion

Aerospace and Aeronautical Engineering

This area of study produces graduates whose specialized skills are in high demand. The purpose of aerospace engineering is to develop aerospace vehicles. It includes knowledge from many areas such as electrical and chemical engineering, design, structure, and analysis of materials. A high number of graduates move into military service as engineering officers; many others find employment in the aerospace industry.

COURSE REQUIREMENTS

Aerodynamics	Propulsion
Aeroelasticity	Space Technology
Aerospace Materials	Structural Dynamics
Aerothermochemistry	Superaerodynamics
High Speed Aerodynamics	Vehicle Design
Numerical Methods	Viscous Fluids
Numerical Simulation	

OPTIONS WITHIN MAJOR

Aerodynamics	Propulsion
Design	Testing

RECOMMENDED HIGH SCHOOL COURSES

Chemistry	Math (3 years)
English	Physics

The Career Connection for College Education

CAREERS	D.O.T. NUMBER	OUTLOOK	AVERAGE INITIAL SALARY
Bachelor Degrees			
Aerodynamicist	002.061-010	Good/Exc.	$30,600
Aeronautical-Design Engineer	002.061-022	Excellent	31,000
Aeronautical Engineer	002.061-014	Excellent	32,400
Aeronautical Stress Analyst	002.061-030	Good	27,400
Aeronautical-Test Engineer	002.061-018	Good	25,700
Graduate Degrees			
Aeronautical Engineer	002.061-014	Excellent	38,900
Professor	090.227-010	Good	32,900
Aeronautical-Research Engineer	002.061-026	Excellent	39,000

Occupational Personality Styles: Scientific, Technical

DPT Functions: Data = H   People = L   Things = H

GOE Work Groups: Engineering, Engineering Technology

African Studies

African studies is an interdisciplinary program typically referred to as "area studies." It integrates ideas and principles from anthropology, literature, history, geography, and economics. This broadly based education allows one to do historical research, social, political, and economic analysis, and literary criticism. Students often continue on to advanced studies in law, business administration, or liberal arts, or may become involved in teaching or government service.

COURSE REQUIREMENTS

Africa and Early Man
African Art
African Roots in America
Archaeology of Africa
Central Africa
Colonization of Africa
Cultural Anthropology
Cultures of Africa
East Africa
Economics of Africa

Folklore Medicine
Geography of Africa
Inter-African Relations
Mediterranean Africa
Political Thought
Racial Issues
Social Anthropology
South Africa
Uncommon Languages
Wildlife of Africa

OPTIONS WITHIN MAJOR

Anthropology
Geography

Political Science

RECOMMENDED HIGH SCHOOL COURSES

Art
Economics
English
Foreign Language

Geography
History
Literature

CAREERS	D.O.T. NUMBER	OUTLOOK	AVERAGE INITIAL SALARY
Bachelor Degrees			
Biographer	052.067-010	Fair/Poor	Varies
Correspondent	131.267-018	Fair	$24,000
Foreign-Service Officer	188.117-106	Fair	25,100
Historian	052.067-022	Fair/Poor	25,200
Import/Export Agent	184.117-022	Good	23,100
Intelligence Expert	059.267-010	Good/Exc.	25,900
Public Relations Specialist	165.167-014	Fair	29,100
Publications Editor	132.037-022	Poor	25,300
Travel Agent	252.152-010	Good	17,200
Graduate Degrees			
Foreign Service	051.067-010	Good	30,200
Professor	090.227-010	Good	32,900
Researcher	199.267-034	Good	30,000

Occupational Personality Styles: Social, Scientific

DPT Functions: Data = H   People = M   Things = L

GOE Work Group: Social Research

Agricultural Economics

Agricultural economics and agribusiness management are a synthesis of training in economics, scientific agriculture, business management, accounting, and finance. Graduates find employment opportunities in farm and ranch management, banking, transportation, food processing, farm equipment and products, real estate, food retailing, and other related agribusiness firms. Both governmental agencies and private firms need graduates in this major who are able to work on the improvement of agricultural products, marketing, and distribution.

COURSE REQUIREMENTS

Accounting and Finance
Agribusiness Finance
Agribusiness Mgt. Economics
Agricultural Marketing
Agronomy and Horticulture
Animal Science
Computer Science
Demand and Price Analysis
Economics and Agriculture

Farm and Ranch Management
Food Science
Futures Trading
Land and Range Economics
Mathematics and Statistics
Micro/Macroeconomics Theory
Public Policy
Real Estate Appraisal and Finance
Research Methods

OPTIONS WITHIN MAJOR

Agribusiness
Agricultural Economics
Farm and Ranch Management

Food Industries Management
Real Estate

RECOMMENDED HIGH SCHOOL COURSES

Accounting
Agriculture
Botany
Business/Economics

Chemistry
Math
Vocational Agriculture

The Career Connection for College Education

CAREERS	D.O.T. NUMBER	OUTLOOK	AVERAGE INITIAL SALARY
Associate Degrees			
Agribusiness Technologist		Fair	$18,400
Agricultural Supplier		Good	16,500
Farm Manager	096.127-018	Poor	22,600
Farm Real Estate Salesperson	186.167-054	Fair	23,000
Food Service Agent	906.683-010	Good	15,000
Food Retailer Distributor		Fair	16,500
Bachelor Degrees			
Agricultural Agent	096.127-014	Fair	23,500
Agricultural Appraiser	188.167-014	Good	22,000
Claims Adjuster	241.217-010	Fair/Good	20,000
Extension Service Specialist	096.127-014	Good	20,000
Farm Management Adviser	096.127-018	Fair	23,000
Market Research Analyst	050.067-014	Good/Exc.	25,100
Rural Bank Manager	186.167-078	Good	27,000
Teacher	091.221-010	Fair	19,500
Graduate Degrees			
Agribusiness Management		Good	28,200
Agricultural Agent	096.127-014	Fair	27,000
Agricultural Economist	050.067-010	Good/Fair	28,000
Market/Data Analyst	045.107-030	Good	25,700
Professor	090.227-010	Good	32,900

Occupational Personality Styles: Scientific, Technical

DPT Functions: Data = H   People = M   Things = L

GOE Work Groups: Life Sciences, Mathematics and Statistics, Social Research

Agronomy

Agronomists are scientists who face the challenge of solving man's most critical world problem: providing enough food for mankind. Basic principles of the biological and physical sciences are applied to the management of soils and the production of food, fiber, and ornamental plants by the agronomist. Private industry and government agencies provide a good job market.

COURSE REQUIREMENTS

Animal Science
Botany
Chemistry
College Algebra
Crop Ecology
Crop Science
Field Crop Production

Irrigated Soils
Nursery Science
Pest Management
Soil Fertility
Soil Science
Water Resources

OPTIONS WITHIN MAJOR

Agribusiness
Management Advisory Services

Production

RECOMMENDED HIGH SCHOOL COURSES

Botany
Business
Chemistry

English
Math
Vocational Agriculture

CAREERS	D.O.T. NUMBER	OUTLOOK	AVERAGE INITIAL SALARY
Associate Degree			
Sales Representative	272.357-010	Good	$19,200
Bachelor Degrees			
Agricultural Agent	096.127-014	Fair	23,600
Agricultural Engineer	013.061-010	Fair	28,900
Agronomist	040.061-010	Good	23,100
Land/Water Use Analyst	029.081-010	Fair/Good	22,000
Range Manager	040.061-046	Fair	17,900
Soil Scientist	040.061-058	Good	22,500
Soil/Water Conservationist	040.061-054	Fair	20,900
Teacher	091.227-010	Fair/Good	19,500
Graduate Degrees			
Professor	090.227-010	Good	32,900
Researcher	199.267-034	Good	33,100

Occupational Personality Styles: Scientific, Technical

DPT Functions: Data = H   People = L   Things = M

GOE Work Groups: Life Sciences, Managerial Work: Plants and Animals

American Studies

American studies is an interdisciplinary program typically referred to as "area studies." It integrates ideas and principles from anthropology, literature, history, geography, and economics. This broadly based education allows one to do historical research, social, political, and economic analysis, and literary criticism. Students often continue on to advanced studies in law, business administration, or liberal arts, or may become involved in teaching or government service.

COURSE REQUIREMENTS

American Architecture
American Art
American Family History
American Novel
American Political Thought
Archaeology
Canadian-American Relations
Cultures of North America
Ecology
Economic History of North America
Economic Thought

Economics of Energy and Environment
Folklife and Folklore
Geography of North America
Hispanic Southwest
Inter-American Relations
Modern American Language Usage
Motion Pictures in America
Native Peoples of North America
Themes in American Literature
Urban Government

OPTIONS WITHIN MAJOR

Business
Culture

Economics
Politics

RECOMMENDED HIGH SCHOOL COURSES

Art
Economics
English
Foreign Language

Geography
History
Literature

CAREERS	D.O.T. NUMBER	OUTLOOK	AVERAGE INITIAL SALARY
Bachelor Degrees			
Biographer	052.067-010	Fair/Poor	Varies
Correspondent	131.267-018	Fair	$24,000
Foreign-Service Officer	188.117-106	Fair	25,100
Historian	052.067-022	Fair/Poor	25,200
Import/Export Agent	184.117-022	Good	23,100
Intelligence Expert	059.267-010	Good/Exc.	25,900
Public Relations Specialist	165.167-014	Fair	29,100
Publications Editor	132.037-022	Poor	25,300
Travel Agent	252.152-018	Good	17,200
Graduate Degrees			
Foreign Service	051.067-010	Good	30,200
Professor	090.227-010	Good	32,900
Researcher	199.267-034	Good	30,000

Occupational Personality Styles:	Social, Scientific
DPT Functions:	Data = H People = M Things = L
GOE Work Group:	Social Research

Animal Science

Animal science provides a combination of classroom teaching, laboratory studies, and practical experience in the study of animals that serve mankind. Graduates develop skills applying to the production and management of meat, dairy, and food industries; meat packing and production; practical livestock farming and management; swine, poultry, beef, dairy, or sheep operations; consulting and field work; and preveterinary medicine. Although a majority of the graduates become self-employed, others seek employment with government agencies, pharmaceutical companies, civil agencies, or colleges and universities (teaching and research).

COURSE REQUIREMENTS

Accounting
Agricultural Economics
Agronomy
Animal Anatomy
Animal Breeding
Animal Hygiene
Animal Physiology
Animal Physiology and Anatomy
Applied Animal Nutrition
Chemistry
Feeds and Feeding
Horse Production
Horticulture
Livestock Evaluation
Math
Meat Processing
Milk and Milk Products
Poultry Production
Veterinary Pharmacology

OPTIONS WITHIN MAJOR

Business and Industry
Preveterinary
Production
Science

RECOMMENDED HIGH SCHOOL COURSES

Agriculture
Algebra
Biology
Chemistry
English (3 years)
Geometry
Vocational Agriculture

CAREERS	D.O.T. NUMBER	OUTLOOK	AVERAGE INITIAL SALARY
Associate Degrees			
Cattle Rancher	410.161-018	Fair/Poor	$20,200
Dairy Manager	180.167-026	Fair/Poor	23,500
Federal Meat Grader		Fair/Poor	15,200
Food and Meat Inspector	168.267-042	Fair	16,200
Poultry Manager	180.167-046	Fair	20,000
Bachelor Degrees			
Dairy Technologist	040.061-022	Good/Fair	24,100
Livestock Extension Agent	096.127-010	Fair/Good	22,800
Graduate Degrees			
Animal Scientist	040.061-014	Good	30,000
Dairy Scientist	040.061-018	Fair	29,600
Geneticist	041.061-050	Good	24,600
Poultry Scientist	040.061-042	Fair	24,600
Professor	090.227-010	Good	32,900
Research and Development	040.061-042	Good	30,000

Occupational Personality Styles:	Scientific, Technical
DPT Functions:	Data = H People = L Things = H
GOE Work Groups:	Life Sciences, Managerial Work: Plants and Animals

Anthropology

Anthropologists study the world's varied peoples and their cultures. They want to know how and why the variety arose. They also seek the similarities we all share—our human nature. Social and cultural anthropologists study living peoples in all aspects of their lives—economic and technological, social, political, aesthetic, religious, and so on. Social anthropologists emphasize the importance of social arrangements as determiners of differences and similarities. Cultural anthropologists emphasize culture, consisting of the customary thinking and feeling patterns with the world and themselves. Archaeologists are mainly the anthropologists of the peoples no longer living; they excavate and interpret earlier cultures and societies from their material remains. Linguistic, biological, and psychological anthropologists specialize in particular bodies of information and certain methods, but all of them are still concerned with differences. The breadth of this subject makes it exceptionally valuable as liberal education preparation for a profession or for life; however, graduate work to at least the master level is important in securing most employment in the field.

COURSE REQUIREMENTS

Ancient Cultures
Archaeological Methods
Biological Anthropology
Economic Institutions
Field Archaeology
Human Osteology
Intercultural Communications

Moral and Ritual Institutions
Museology
Old World Civilization
Psychological Anthropology
Social Anthropology
Theory of Archaeology

OPTIONS WITHIN MAJOR

Applied Anthropology
Archaeology

Museology

RECOMMENDED HIGH SCHOOL COURSES

English (4 years)
Geography
History

Humanities
Literature

CAREERS	D.O.T. NUMBER	OUTLOOK	AVERAGE INITIAL SALARY
Bachelor Degrees			
Archaeological Technician		Fair	$16,300
Museum Technician	102.381-010	Fair	16,300
Graduate Degrees			
Anthropologist	055.067-010	Fair	27,200
Applied Anthropologist	055.067-014	Fair	27,000
Archaeologist	055.067-018	Good	26,900
Archivist	101.167-010	Good	24,600
Consultant/Researcher		Fair	25,900
Cultural Anthropologist	055.067-010	Fair	27,200
Ethnologist	055.067-022	Good	27,000
Linguist	059.067-014	Fair/Good	27,300
Museum Curator	102.017-010	Fair/Good	27,900
Physical or Social Anthropologist	055.067-014	Fair	27,000
Professor	090.227-010	Fair	32,900

Occupational Personality Styles: Scientific, Technical

DPT Functions: Data = H   People = L   Things = H

GOE Work Group: Social Research

Architecture

Architects provide a wide variety of professional services to individuals, organizations, corporations, or government agencies planning a building project. Architects are involved in all phases of development of a building project, from the initial discussion of general ideas through construction. Their duties require a variety of skills—design, engineering, managerial, and supervisory.

Most architects work for architectural firms, builders, real estate firms, or other businesses that have large construction programs. Some work for government agencies responsible for housing, planning, or community development. Employment opportunities are also found in the federal government, mainly for the Departments of Defense, Interior, Housing and Urban Development, and the General Services Administration.

COURSE REQUIREMENTS

Architectural History	Fine Arts
Architectural Theory	Geometry
Calculus	Graphics
Design	Physics
Economics	Structural Elements
Engineering and Urban Planning	Urban Design
English	

OPTIONS WITHIN MAJOR

Architecture	Urban Planning

RECOMMENDED HIGH SCHOOL COURSES

Biology	Geometry
Drawing	Mechanical Drawing
English	Public Speaking
General Science	

CAREERS	D.O.T. NUMBER	OUTLOOK	AVERAGE INITIAL SALARY
Bachelor Degrees			
Architect	001.061-010	Good/Exc.	$27,400
Drafter	001.261-010	Excellent	17,600
Marine Architect	001.061-014	Fair	28,200
Urban Planner	199.167-014	Good	24,300
Graduate Degrees			
Architect	001.061-010	Excellent	35,600
Professor	090.227-010	Good	32,900

Occupational Personality Styles: Technical, Artistic

DPT Functions: Data = H   People = L   Things = M

GOE Work Groups: Crafts, Craft Technology

Art

Art and design prepares creative leaders in the visual arts who are sensitive to the aesthetic needs of society. An appreciation for the arts and their importance in the role of the total development of the individual is emphasized. Graduates combine the artistic elements with manufacturing techniques to find employment in industry and economy. Increased leisure time in our society has increased the interest in arts and crafts, and several graduates are able to set up successful studies in ceramics, crafts, painting, printmaking, and sculpting. Despite the competition in some areas, graduates are also successful in obtaining jobs in education.

COURSE REQUIREMENTS

American Art
Art History
Business Practices
Ceramics
Contemporary Art
Drawing
Greek Art
Hand Lettering

Medieval Art
Philosophy of Fine Arts
Printmaking
Recreational Arts and Crafts
Sculpture
Survey of Architecture
Watercolor

OPTIONS WITHIN MAJOR

Art Education
Art History
Ceramics
Drawing

Painting
Printmaking
Sculpture
Studio Art

RECOMMENDED HIGH SCHOOL COURSES

Art

Design

The Career Connection for College Education

CAREERS	D.O.T. NUMBER	OUTLOOK	AVERAGE INITIAL SALARY
Bachelor Degrees			
Advertising Designer	247.387-018	Good	$19,200
Art Therapist	076.127-010	Fair	18,000
Audiovisual Production Specialist	149.061-010	Fair/Good	20,100
Cartoonist	141.061-010	Fair	15,100
Copy Artist	144.061-022	Fair	17,300
Fashion Artist	141.061-014	Good	21,200
Furniture Designer	142.061-022	Fair	17,900
Illustrator	141.061-022	Good	19,300
Layout Designer	141.061-018	Good	19,000
Medical Illustrator	141.061-026	Good	25,000
Quick Sketch Artist	149.041-010	Fair	15,600
Sculptor	144.061-018	Fair	Varies
Set Designer	142.061-050	Fair	19,800
Studio Artist	144.061-010	Fair	Varies
Teacher, Elementary (Secondary)	149.021-010	Good	19,500
Graduate Degrees			
Art Director	188.117-042	Fair	49,600
Professor	090.227-010	Good	32,900

Occupational Personality Styles:	Artistic, Influencing
DPT Functions:	Data = H People = L Things = H
GOE Work Groups:	Craft Arts, Performing Arts: Dance, Performing Arts: Drama, Performing Arts: Music, Visual Arts

Asian Studies

Asian studies is an interdisciplinary program typically referred to as "area studies." It integrates ideas and principles from anthropology, literature, history, geography, and economics. This broadly based education allows one to do historical research, social, political, and economic analysis, and literary criticism. Students often continue on to advanced studies in law, business administration, or liberal arts, or may become involved in teaching or government service.

COURSE REQUIREMENTS

Asian and International Politics
Asian Culture
Asian Literature
Asian Political Thought
Asian Religions and Thought
Business and Culture
Chinese Law
Chinese Literature
Economic Development
History of Asia
Humanities in Asia

International Business
International Trade and Finance
Japanese Law
Japanese Literature
Korean Law
Korean Literature
Modern Asia
Oriental Art and Architecture
Oriental Mythology
Social Sciences in Asia

OPTIONS WITHIN MAJOR

Business
Economics
Government

Philosophy
Politics

RECOMMENDED HIGH SCHOOL COURSES

Art
Economics
English
Foreign Language

Geography
History
Literature

CAREERS	D.O.T. NUMBER	OUTLOOK	AVERAGE INITIAL SALARY
Bachelor Degrees			
Biographer	052.067-010	Fair/Poor	Varies
Correspondent	131.267-018	Fair	$24,000
Foreign-Service Officer	188.117-106	Fair	25,100
Historian	052.067-022	Fair/Poor	25,200
Import/Export Agent	184.117-022	Good	23,100
Intelligence Expert	059.267-010	Good/Exc.	25,900
Public Relations Specialist	165.167-014	Fair	29,100
Publications Editor	132.037-022	Poor	25,300
Travel Agent	252.152-010	Good	17,200
Graduate Degrees			
Foreign Service	051.067-010	Good	30,200
Professor	090.227-010	Good	32,900
Researcher	199.267-034	Good	30,000

Occupational Personality Styles: Social, Scientific

DPT Functions: Data = H   People = M   Things = L

GOE Work Group: Social Research

Botany

Agricultural and ecological problems in the world will be solved, in part, by those with in-depth knowledge of botany. Development of plant hybrids that are disease-resistant and produce a high plant yield will be a fundamental part of world prosperity and cultural mobility. Botany offers professional training in a wide variety of careers including governmental services, research institutions, and industry.

COURSE REQUIREMENTS

Animal Science
Biochemistry
Biology
Botany
Chemistry
Ecology
Genetics
Math

Microbiology
Plant Anatomy
Plant Classification
Plant Cytology
Plant Geography
Plant Pathology
Plant Physiology

OPTIONS WITHIN MAJOR

Disease Control
Farming Research
Forestry

Genetics
Governmental Agencies
Range Science

RECOMMENDED HIGH SCHOOL COURSES

Biology
Botany
Chemistry

English
Math (3 years)

The Career Connection for College Education

CAREERS	D.O.T. NUMBER	OUTLOOK	AVERAGE INITIAL SALARY
Bachelor Degrees			
Botanist	041.061-038	Fair/Poor	$23,500
Plant Breeder	041.061-082	Fair	20,900
Graduate Degrees			
Geneticist	041.061-050	Good	24,600
Nematologist	041.061-066	Fair	25,000
Plant Cytologist	041.061-042	Good	28,600
Plant Pathologist	041.061-086	Good	30,500

Occupational Personality Styles: Scientific, Technical

DPT Functions: Data = H   People = L   Things = M

GOE Work Groups: Life Sciences, Managerial Work: Plants and Animals

Business Education

Business education teachers are qualified to teach office skills, business economics, bookkeeping, and related office or clerical subjects. Related to office education is socio-business and distributive education, in which students are instructed in sales, promotion, buying operations, market research communications, and management. Many business education majors are qualified for work in the business community as well as teaching in secondary schools. Vocational programs are expanding across the nation, and the employment prospects for business teachers should remain positive.

COURSE REQUIREMENTS

Business Communications
Business Law
Business Policy
Computer Science
Economics
Elementary Accounting

Financial Management
General College Math
Marketing Management
Operations Management
Statistics

OPTIONS WITHIN MAJOR

Business
Distributive Education

Office Education

RECOMMENDED HIGH SCHOOL COURSES

Business
English (4 years)

Math (3 years)
Typing

CAREERS	D.O.T. NUMBER	OUTLOOK	AVERAGE INITIAL SALARY
Bachelor Degrees			
Administrative Assistant	169.167-010	Excellent	$17,000
Office Manager	186.117-034	Good/Exc.	19,500
Teacher	091.227-010	Good/Exc.	19,500
Graduate Degrees			
Business Consultant	189.167-010	Good/Exc.	39,200
Professor	090.227-010	Good/Exc.	32,900

Occupational Personality Styles: Detail-oriented, Social

DPT Functions: Data = H   People = H   Things = L

GOE Work Groups: Administrative Detail, Clerical Machine Operation, Clerical Handling, Contracts and Claims, Records Processing

Business Management

Business management programs are designed to prepare students for responsible leadership in their chosen profession by providing in-depth training and experience in marketing, production, finance, individual and group behavior, and other management skills. Occupational opportunities for graduates in this field remain positive throughout the country in both government and private industry. Besides preparing for management and administration of business, many students go on to study law or Master of Business Administration programs.

COURSE REQUIREMENTS

Accounting	Marketing
Business Computing	Microeconomics
Business Mathematics	Operations Analysis
Business Policy	Operations Management
Buying Behavior	Organizational Behavior
Commercial Law	Public Policy
Financial Management	Real Estate
General College Math	Retailing
Investments	Risk Management
Macroeconomics	Statistics

OPTIONS WITHIN MAJOR

General Business	Operating/Systems Analysis
Finance	Retailing
Marketing	

RECOMMENDED HIGH SCHOOL COURSES

English (4 years)	Math (3 years)
General Science	

CAREERS	D.O.T. NUMBER	OUTLOOK	AVERAGE INITIAL SALARY
Bachelor Degrees			
Banker	186.167-070	Good	$25,000
Broker	162.157-018	Good/Exc.	34,000
Budget/Management Analyst	160.162-022	Good/Exc.	25,100
Buyer	162.157-018	Fair/Good	24,500
Credit Manager	186.167-086	Good	23,500
IRS Agent		Good	21,500
Job Analyst	166.267-018	Good	20,000
Labor Relations Manager	166.167-034	Fair	30,600
Market Research Analyst	050.067-014	Good/Exc.	25,100
Personnel Manager	166.167-018	Excellent	30,700
Placement Director	166.267-010	Good	27,800
Purchasing Agent	162.157-038	Good/Fair	25,100
Retail Manager	185.167-046	Good/Exc.	23,000
Sales Manager	163.167-018	Good	23,900
Stockbroker	250.257-018	Good/Exc.	34,100
Graduate Degrees			
Airport Manager	184.117-026	Fair	31,000
Director of Public Service	184.117-010	Fair	28,100
Director of Transportation	184.117-014	Fair	27,000
Management Analyst	161.167-010	Excellent	30,100
Market Research Analyst	050.067-014	Excellent	41,600
Professor	090.227-010	Good	32,900
Systems Analyst	030.167-014	Excellent	33,000

Occupational Personality Styles: Influencing, Social, Detail-oriented

DPT Functions: Data = H   People = H   Things = L

GOE Work Groups: Business Administration, Business Management, Finance, General Sales, Hospitality Services, Promotion, Sales Technology

Canadian Studies

Canadian studies is an interdisciplinary program typically referred to as "area studies." It integrates ideas and principles from anthropology, literature, history, geography, and economics. This broadly based education allows one to do historical research, social, political, and economic analysis, and literary criticism. Students often continue on to advanced studies in law, business administration, or liberal arts, or may become involved in teaching or government service.

COURSE REQUIREMENTS

American Architecture
American Art
Archaeology of North America
Canadian Educational System
Canadian Foreign Policy
Canadian Political Issues
Canadian Political Thought
Canadian Society
Canadian-United States Relations

Cultures of Canada
Ecology
Economic History of North America
Economic Thought
Folklife and Folklore
Geography of North America
International Business
International Communications
Native Peoples of North America

OPTIONS WITHIN MAJOR

Business
Economics

Politics

RECOMMENDED HIGH SCHOOL COURSES

Art
Economics
English
Foreign Language

Geography
History
Literature

CAREERS	D.O.T. NUMBER	OUTLOOK	AVERAGE INITIAL SALARY
Bachelor Degrees			
Biographer	052.067-010	Fair/Poor	Varies
Correspondent	131.267-018	Fair	$24,000
Foreign-Service Officer	188.117-106	Fair	25,100
Historian	052.067-022	Fair/Poor	25,200
Import/Export Agent	184.117-022	Good	23,100
Intelligence Expert	059.267-010	Good/Exc.	25,900
Public Relations Specialist	165.167-014	Fair	29,100
Publications Editor	132.037-022	Poor	25,300
Travel Agent	252.152-010	Good	17,200
Graduate Degrees			
Foreign Service	051.067-010	Good	30,200
Professor	090.227-010	Good	32,900
Researcher	199.267-034	Good	30,000

Occupational Personality Styles: Social, Scientific

DPT Functions: Data = H   People = M   Things = L

GOE Work Group: Social Research

Chemical Engineering

The chemical engineer's principal activity is changing raw materials into useful and valuable products, and as such they are widely employed applying these principles of chemical research and engineering to production and processing operations. Virtually all qualified graduates find employment in some form of research, design, operation, or management, especially as it deals with current problems such as energy or pollution. The chemical engineering technician assists the chemical engineer in all industries by obtaining and analyzing data, operating equipment, and planning and carrying out experiments. Most technicians find employment in areas such as industrial design, environmental engineering, and related research and developmental projects.

COURSE REQUIREMENTS

Analytical Geometry
Applied Ordinary Differential
   Equations
Calculus
Chemical Engineering
Chemical Engineering Kinetics
Chemical Engineering
   Thermodynamics
Chemical Process Principles
Elements of Electrical Engineering

Engineering Mechanics—Statics
Fundamentals of Physics
Organic Chemistry
Physical Chemistry
Plant Design and Economics
Principles of Chemistry
Process Synthesis
Science of Engineering Metals
Unit Operations

OPTIONS WITHIN MAJOR

Bioengineering
Energy and Environment
Management

Nuclear Engineering
Research
Semiconductor Fabrication

RECOMMENDED HIGH SCHOOL COURSES

Chemistry
Drafting
Industrial Shop

Math (3 years)
Physics

CAREERS	D.O.T. NUMBER	OUTLOOK	AVERAGE INITIAL SALARY
Associate Degrees			
Chemical Engineer Technician	008.261-010	Good/Exc.	$19,300
Chemical Operator	558.685-062	Fair/Good	17,700
Laboratory Tester	022.281-018	Fair/Good	18,200
Bachelor Degrees			
Chemical Design Engineer	008.061-014	Fair/Good	28,900
Chemical Engineer	008.061-018	Good/Exc.	31,700
Chemical Equipment Engineer	008.151-010	Fair/Good	27,100
Chemical Operator	559.382-018	Fair	24,500
Environmental Health Scientist	029.081-010	Excellent	28,000
Nuclear Engineer	015.061-014	Excellent	31,000
Graduate Degrees			
Biomedical Engineer	019.061-010	Excellent	38,700
Engineer	008.061-018	Fair/Good	38,900
Petroleum Engineer	010.061-018	Good/Exc.	35,000
Professor	090.227-010	Fair/Good	32,900
Researcher	008.061-022	Good/Exc.	38,900

Occupational Personality Styles: Scientific, Technical

DPT Functions: Data = H   People = L   Things = M

GOE Work Groups: Engineering, Physical Sciences

Chemistry

Chemistry is the study of matter and the manner in which it changes and reacts as well as the laws governing those reactions. Chemists develop and simplify models and theories and perform research in biochemistry, geochemistry, organic chemistry, analytical chemistry, inorganic chemistry, and physical chemistry. Employment opportunities in chemistry are excellent. Qualified, creative graduates find employment teaching or performing research in virtually any industry.

COURSE REQUIREMENTS

Analytical Chemistry
Analytical Geometry
Biochemistry
Biophysical Chemistry
Calculus
Chemical Literature
Chemistry
Computer Programming
Inorganic Chemistry
Instrumental Analysis

Organic Chemistry
Organic Compounds
Physical Chemistry
Physics
Physiological Chemistry
Principles of Chemistry
Principles of Physics
Qualitative Analysis
Quantitative Analysis
Scientific Computing

OPTIONS WITHIN MAJOR

Analytical Chemistry
Biochemistry
Inorganic Chemistry

Organic Chemistry
Physical Chemistry

RECOMMENDED HIGH SCHOOL COURSES

Chemistry
English (4 years)

Math (all available courses)
Physics

CAREERS	D.O.T. NUMBER	OUTLOOK	AVERAGE INITIAL SALARY
Associate Degrees			
Chemical Lab Technician	022.261-010	Fair	$18,500
Chemical Operator	559.382-018	Fair	17,700
Laboratory Tester	022.281-018	Fair	18,200
Bachelor Degrees			
Assayer	022.261-010	Fair	21,200
Chemical Laboratory Chief	022.161-010	Fair	26,400
Chemical Operator	559.382-018	Fair	21,800
Chemical Technologist	078.261-010	Good	21,500
Chemist	022.061-010	Excellent	26,800
Criminologist	054.067-014	Fair/Good	24,000
Science Writer	131.267-026	Good	26,500
Soil Scientist	040.061-058	Good	22,500
Teacher	091.227-010	Fair	19,500
Graduate Degrees			
Biochemist	041.061-026	Good	28,900
Production Chemist	022.061-010	Good	26,200
Professor	090.227-010	Good	32,900
Research Chemist	022.061-010	Good	38,800

Occupational Personality Style:	Scientific
DPT Functions:	Data = H People = L Things = H
GOE Work Groups:	Physical Sciences, Mathematics and Statistics

Chinese

The study of Chinese literature and language prepares graduates with a cultural understanding of and ability to communicate with people in Asian lands. Increased international commerce, research, and interaction have created a need for people well trained in Chinese language, literature, and thought. Apart from practical language applications in government and literary work, several graduates find teaching opportunities on the college level.

COURSE REQUIREMENTS

Chinese
Composition
Conversation
Cultural Civilization

Grammar
Literature
Phonetics
Translation

OPTIONS WITHIN MAJOR

Business
Education

Translation

RECOMMENDED HIGH SCHOOL COURSES

Foreign Language
Geography
History

Humanities
Literature

CAREERS	D.O.T. NUMBER	OUTLOOK	AVERAGE INITIAL SALARY
Bachelor Degrees			
Customs Official	168.267-022	Fair	$16,500
Foreign-Service Officer	188.117-106	Fair	24,000
Import/Export Agent	184.117-022	Good	25,100
Intelligence Expert	059.267-010	Good	25,200
Interpreter	137.267-014	Fair/Good	23,100
Language Researcher	059.067-014	Fair	25,900
Public Relations Specialist	165.167-014	Fair	29,100
Scientific Writer	131.267-026	Fair	25,300
Teacher	019.227-010	Poor	19,500
Translator	137.267-018	Good	20,000
Travel Agent	252.152-010	Good	17,200
Graduate Degrees			
Professor	090.227-010	Good	32,900
Scientific Linguist	059.067-014	Fair	27,300

Occupational Personality Styles: Scientific, Social

DPT Functions: Data = H   People = M   Things = L

GOE Work Groups: Business Administration, Business Management, Educational and Library Services, Security Services

Civil Engineering

Combining a knowledge of mathematics, chemistry, and physics, the civil engineer develops means to utilize the materials and forces of nature in the design and construction of structures, pollution control, and other engineering endeavors. The civil engineering technician assists the engineer in providing facilities and structures for the community, industry, and government. A shortage of civil engineers and the need for solutions to technical problems (waste disposal, mass transportation, urban growth) will continue to increase job possibilities for civil engineering graduates.

COURSE REQUIREMENTS

Analytical Geometry
Calculus
Civil Engineering Design
Elementary Soil Mechanics
Elements of Electrical Engineering
Engineering Graphics
Engineering Mechanics–Dynamics
Engineering Mechanics–Statics
Engineering Seminar
Engineering Surveying
Geology for Engineers
Highway Engineering
Hydraulic Engineering
Hydraulics and Fluid Flow History
Hydrology
Introduction to Civil Engineering
Microbiology
Principles of Physics
Professional, Legal, and Economic
  Problems in Engineering
Properties of Materials
Structural Steel/Reinforced
  Concrete Design
Structural Theory

OPTIONS WITHIN MAJOR

Environmental Engineering
Geotechnical Engineering
Highway and Transportation
  Engineering
Solid Mechanics
Water Resources

RECOMMENDED HIGH SCHOOL COURSES

Algebra
Calculus
Chemistry
Geometry
Physics

CAREERS	D.O.T. NUMBER	OUTLOOK	AVERAGE INITIAL SALARY
Associate Degree			
Civil Engineering Technician	005.261-014	Good/Exc.	$21,500
Bachelor Degrees			
Airport Engineer	005.061-010	Good	29,000
Civil Engineer	005.061-014	Excellent	33,400
Construction Engineer	005.061-034	Excellent	26,000
Highway Engineer	005.061-038	Good	25,100
Hydraulic Engineer	005.061-018	Good	29,000
Irrigation Engineer	005.061-022	Fair/Poor	23,000
Sanitation Engineer	005.061-030	Good/Exc.	28,500
Structural Engineer	005.061-034	Excellent	28,900
Transportation Engineer	005.061-038	Good	28,000
Graduate Degrees			
Professor	090.227-010	Good	32,900
Research and Development	199.267-034	Good	36,700

Occupational Personality Styles: Scientific, Technical

DPT Functions: Data = H   People = L   Things = H

GOE Work Groups: Engineering, Business Management

Classical Languages

The multitude of languages in the western world are often related to the original classical languages, Greek and Latin. Study of these languages is essential for biblical and early Christian studies, romance philosophy, or studies of ancient history and comparative literature. Many students contemplating graduate work in linguistics or the professional school of law, medicine, and dentistry find the classical languages an advantageous undergraduate study. Teaching positions are available in Latin, but Greek is essentially used on the collegiate level.

COURSE REQUIREMENTS

Classical Greek Culture
Grammar and Composition
Greek and Latin Masterpieces
   in English Translation
Greek and Roman Mythology
   in English Translation
Greek Drama in English
   Translation
Greek Reading/Composition

Latin
Latin Culture
Latin Literature
Latin Stylistic/Literary Analysis
Masterpieces of Greek
   Literature
Masterpieces of Latin
   Literature

OPTIONS WITHIN MAJOR

Classical Civilization
Greek

Latin

RECOMMENDED HIGH SCHOOL COURSES

Humanities
Language

Literature

CAREERS	D.O.T. NUMBER	OUTLOOK	AVERAGE INITIAL SALARY
Bachelor Degrees			
Archivist	101.167-010	Fair	$25,100
Genealogist	052.067-018	Poor/Fair	20,100
Intelligence Expert	059.267-010	Fair/Good	25,200
Research Assistant	109.267-010	Fair/Good	20,400
Teacher	091.227-010	Fair	19,500
Translator	137.267-018	Fair/Good	20,000
Graduate Degrees			
Anthropologist	055.067-010	Fair	27,700
Archaeologist	055.067-018	Good	26,900
Historian	052.067-022	Fair/Poor	Varies
Professor	090.227-010	Fair	32,900
Scientific Linguist	059.067-014	Good	27,300

Occupational Personality Style: Scientific

DPT Functions: Data = H   People = M   Things = L

GOE Work Group: Social Research

Clothing and Textiles

Clothing and textiles deals with the wise selection, effective use, and proper care of clothes in order to meet the needs of individuals and to provide training in the textile and apparel industries. Careers are open in demonstration work, designing, dressmaking, fashion illustration, merchandising, promotion, purchasing, manufacturing, textile testing, and theatrical costuming. Graduate work is also available for those interested in college teaching, research, or extension services. Employment opportunities are usually available in metropolitan areas with large department stores or other large clothing and textile firms.

COURSE REQUIREMENTS

Apparel Design
Apparel Evaluation
Children's Clothing
Clothing and Human Behavior
Clothing Construction
Clothing Merchandising
Dress and Pattern
Economy, Society, and Public
    Policy
Elementary College Chemistry
Fashion Illustration
Fashion Industry
Fitting
Flat Pattern Design
General Psychology
General Textiles
History of Costume
Mass Production Techniques
Personal Fashion Selection
Selection and Care
Tailoring
Textiles
Weaving

OPTIONS WITHIN MAJOR

Fashion Design
Fashion Merchandising
General Clothing and Textiles

RECOMMENDED HIGH SCHOOL COURSES

Chemistry
Home Economics
Sewing

CAREERS	D.O.T. NUMBER	OUTLOOK	AVERAGE INITIAL SALARY
Bachelor Degrees			
Buyer	162.157-018	Good	$24,500
Clothes Designer	142.061-018	Fair/Good	18,300
Extension Service Specialist	096.127-014	Good	20,000
Fashion Coordinator	185.157-010	Excellent	23,400
Fashion Designer	142.061-018	Fair	21,900
Fashion Illustrator	141.061-014	Fair	19,900
Fashion Promoter	096.121-014	Fair	22,100
Sales Representative	261.357-010	Good	19,900
Textile Converter	185.167-050	Fair	18,300
Theater Costume Designer	142.061-018	Fair	20,000
Graduate Degree			
Professor	090.227-010	Good	32,900

Occupational Personality Styles:	Influencing, Artistic, Technical
DPT Functions:	Data = H People = M Things = M
GOE Work Groups:	Administrative Detail, Craft Arts, Promotion

Commercial Art, Design, and Photography

Commercial art or design is often a selective program requiring a portfolio that demonstrates past performance. The curriculum itself is performance-based, requiring considerable studio time. The student must expect to show creative work in several areas. In-depth projects in the student's selected specialties are required later in the training. This program is designed to enhance creativity, craftsmanship, and presentation skills on a professional level.

COURSE REQUIREMENTS

Advertising Design
Color Theory
Corporate Identity Design
Environmental Design
Glass Design
Illustration
Industrial Design
Lighting Techniques
Materials and Components
Metal and Jewelry

Packaging and Poster Design
Presentation Models
Problems in Color
Production Drawing
Publication Design
Rendering Techniques
Space Planning
Theory of Environmental Design
Type as Image

OPTIONS WITHIN MAJOR

Crafts Design
Graphic Design
Illustration

Industrial Design
Interior Design
Photography

RECOMMENDED HIGH SCHOOL COURSES

Art
Biology
English
Graphics
Health

Home Economics
Industrial Arts
Math
Social Science

CAREERS	D.O.T. NUMBER	OUTLOOK	AVERAGE INITIAL SALARY
Associate Degrees			
Graphic Artist	979.382-018	Good	$18,200
Photograph Retoucher	976.487-010	Good	15,200
Photographer	143.062-030	Good	21,800
Bachelor Degrees			
Cloth Designer	142.061-014	Fair	20,900
Commercial Designer	141.061-038	Good	21,200
Fashion Artist	141.061-014	Good	21,200
Graphic Designer	141.061-018	Good	20,300
Illustrator	141.061-022	Good	21,800
Industrial Designer	142.061-026	Good	24,900
Interior Designer	142.051-014	Fair	20,200
Set Illustrator	141.061-030	Fair	19,800
Teacher	091.227-010	Fair	19,500
Technical Illustrator	017.281-034	Good	24,500
Graduate Degree			
Professor	090.227-010	Good	32,900

Occupational Personality Styles: Artistic, Technical

DPT Functions: Data = H   People = M   Things = H

GOE Work Group: Craft Arts, Visual Arts

Communications

Communications deals with the effective transmittal of ideas, feelings, and media news. Combining an understanding of the effects of mass media, the behavioral sciences, and communications skills allows the graduate to enter advertising, broadcasting, film making, journalism, government, public relations, speech education, and any career dealing with personal and public communications. Although competition is high for many openings, there is constantly a need for creative, accurate, and effective means of communication.

COURSE REQUIREMENTS

Advertising
Anthropology
Effects of Mass Media
Film
Human Communications
Interpersonal Communications
Journalism
Linguistics
Mass Communications

Methods of Inquiry
Organizational Communications
Photography
Professional Communication
   Experience
Psychology
Public Relations
Sociology
Speech

OPTIONS WITHIN MAJOR

Advertising
Broadcasting
Film Production
Journalism
Journalism Education

Organizational Communications
Photography
Public Relations
Speech

RECOMMENDED HIGH SCHOOL COURSES

English (4 years)
Journalism

Social Science
Speech

The Career Connection for College Education

CAREERS	D.O.T. NUMBER	OUTLOOK	AVERAGE INITIAL SALARY
Associate Degrees			
Motion-Picture Photographer	143.062-022	Fair	$28,600
Photographer	143.062-030	Good	21,800
Photography Director, TV	143.260-010	Good	33,000
Bachelor Degrees			
Advertising Manager	191.167-010	Good	35,500
Copywriter	131.067-014	Good	17,500
Editor	132.067-014	Good	25,200
Journalist	131.067-010	Fair	21,000
Motion-Picture/TV Director	159.167-014	Fair	36,000
Newswriter	131.262-014	Good	22,000
Photojournalist	143.062-034	Fair	21,000
Public Relations Specialist	165.167-014	Good	29,100
Radio/TV Announcer	159.147-010	Fair	18,600
Teacher	091.227-010	Fair/Good	19,500
Graduate Degree			
Professor	090.227-010	Good	32,900

Occupational Personality Styles: Influencing, Social

DPT Functions: Data = H   People = H   Things = L

GOE Work Groups: Communications, Literary Arts, Promotion

Community Health Education

The goal of the health educator is to enhance the physical, mental, and social well-being of the public through planning and implementation of programs that increase public awareness and understanding of health problems and their solutions. The public health educator stimulates local leaders toward appropriate health action; assists schools, hospitals, organizations, and firms in planning health education programs; distributes pamphlets, posters, exhibits, and forms; educates by radio, TV, and press; helps with the evaluation of community health needs; and directs people who need special community services. Employment opportunities are available in private and government health agencies.

COURSE REQUIREMENTS

Advanced First Aid
Community Health
Community Health Education
Consumer Health
Cultural Geography
Drug Use/Abuse
Elementary Human Physiology
Epidemiology
Essentials of Nutrition
Fieldwork in Community Health
First Aid and Safety
Health Education Workshop
Health of the Body System
Health Problems Workshop
Health/Self-Destructive Behavior

Human Physiology
Instructional Media Production
Instructorship in First Aid
Interpersonal Group Process
Medical Sociology
Methods in Health Education
Minority Issues in Community
　　Health Education
Newswriting
Organizational Behavior
Public Relations
Safety Education
Social Analysis
Social Statistics

OPTIONS WITHIN MAJOR

Community Health Education

Public Health Education

RECOMMENDED HIGH SCHOOL COURSES

Art
Biology
Health

Math
Social Sciences

CAREERS	D.O.T. NUMBER	OUTLOOK	AVERAGE INITIAL SALARY
Associate Degrees			
Health Care Center Worker	245.362-014	Fair	$12,500
Health Organization Worker	168.167-018	Good	13,100
Bachelor Degrees			
Community Health Planner	079.167-010	Good/Fair	19,500
Community Health Rep.	079.167-010	Good	19,500
Health Services Adviser	187.117-050	Good/Exc.	19,500
Nutritionist	096.121-014	Good/Exc.	19,000
Graduate Degrees			
Public Health Administrator	079.117-014	Good	27,200
Professor	090.227-010	Good	32,900

Occupational Personality Styles: Social, Serving

DPT Functions: Data = H   People = H   Things = M

GOE Work Group: Regulations Enforcement, Social Services

Computer Science

The computer is being used in nearly every walk of life. Few industries can be found which do not use computers either directly or indirectly. A computer professional must be prepared to deal with the design and implementation of computer systems. Training in computer science varies among basic systems. The current demand for graduates is very high, and the job outlook should remain positive through the next decade.

COURSE REQUIREMENTS

Algorithmic Languages and
   Compilers
Analytical Geometry
   and Calculus
Computer Organization
Computer Organization
   and Programming
Computer Programming
Computers and Society
Digital Logic Design

Discrete Structures
Elementary Mathematical Statistics
Information Structures
Operating Systems Design
Operating Systems Principles
Physics
Programming Languages
Seminar in Computer Science
Topics

OPTIONS WITHIN MAJOR

Programming
Software Engineering

Systems Analysis

RECOMMENDED HIGH SCHOOL COURSES

Algebra
Calculus

Computer Science
Trigonometry

CAREERS	D.O.T. NUMBER	OUTLOOK	AVERAGE INITIAL SALARY
Bachelor Degrees			
Business Programmer	030.162-010	Excellent	$26,500
Computer Operator	213.362-010	Excellent	18,300
Computer Programmer	030.162-010	Excellent	24,100
Information Systems Programmer	007.167-010	Excellent	25,500
Process Control Programmer	020.187-014	Excellent	25,500
Scientific Programmer	030.162-018	Excellent	28,200
Systems Programmer	030.162-022	Excellent	27,500
Technician	003.161-014	Excellent	21,900
Graduate Degrees			
Computer Applications Engineer		Excellent	37,900
Computer Systems Engineer	003.167-026	Excellent	39,000
Systems Analyst	030.167-014	Excellent	33,100

Occupational Personality Styles: Scientific, Technical

DPT Functions: Data = H   People = L   Things = M

GOE Work Group: Mathematics and Statistics

Dance and Physical Education

Currently dance is the fastest growing performing art in the nation, with audiences expanding six-fold and performances increasing seven-fold over the past several years. The quality, vitality, and uniqueness of American dance not only requires traditional skills, but demands imagination, creativity, and true artistic ability. The enthusiasm created among the younger audiences has opened new opportunities for dance majors in teaching, training, and performing.

COURSE REQUIREMENTS

Adaptive/Corrective Physical Ed.
Aerobic Dance
Ballet
Ballroom Dance
Dance Composition
Dance Production
Elementary Human Folk Dance
General Kinesiology

Human Anatomy
Modern Dance
Physiology
Physiology of Activity
Principles of Physical Education
Social Dance
Statistics
Tap Dance

OPTIONS WITHIN MAJOR

Ballet
Dance Specialization

Dance/Sports Combination
Professional Dance

RECOMMENDED HIGH SCHOOL COURSES

Art
Dance

Fine Arts
Sciences

CAREERS	D.O.T. NUMBER	OUTLOOK	AVERAGE INITIAL SALARY
Bachelor Degrees			
Choreographer	151.027-010	Poor	$27,400
Dance Performer	151.047-010	Fair	13,500
Dance Teacher	151.027-014	Good	19,500
Graduate Degree			
Professor	090.227-010	Fair	32,900

Occupational Personality Styles: Artistic, Social, Technical

DPT Functions: Data = M   People = H   Things = M

GOE Work Group: Performing Arts: Dance, Performing Arts: Drama, Educational and Library Services

Dentistry

Because of the shortage of dentists in many areas of the country, dentistry is an excellent health care profession to pursue. Following three or four years of undergraduate work (in a variety of possible majors), students must complete at least four years of professional schooling. Specialization can be considered after graduation.

COURSE REQUIREMENTS

Most students are accepted into dental school with a bachelor's degree including the following courses:

Anatomy	Microbiology
Biochemistry	Organic Chemistry
Calculus	Physics
Chemistry	Physiology
English	Psychology
Genetics	Vertebrate Anatomy

Professional schools are a continuation of the above in more depth and with clinical experiences.

RECOMMENDED HIGH SCHOOL COURSES

Algebra	Geometry
Biology	Physics
English (4 years)	Physiology

CAREERS	D.O.T. NUMBER	OUTLOOK	AVERAGE INITIAL SALARY
Graduate Degrees			
Dentist	072.101-010	Excellent	$ 67,100
Oral Pathologist	072.061-010	Excellent	117,600
Oral Surgeon	072.101-018	Excellent	120,100
Orthodontist	072.101-022	Excellent	112,400
Periodontist	072.101-030	Excellent	102,000
Prosthodontist	072.101-034	Excellent	115,300

Occupational Personality Styles: Scientific, Technical

DPT Functions: Data = H   People = H   Things = H

GOE Work Groups: Life Sciences, Medical Sciences

Design and Illustration

Professionals in these careers play an increasingly important social function in creating corporate, government, and advertising communications. This major is concerned with the organization and combination of format and language. The student spends much time in performance classes and must expect to show creative work in several areas.

COURSE REQUIREMENTS

Advertising Design
Color Theory
Conceptual Drawing
Corporate Identity Design
Design
Environmental Design
Exhibit Design
Graphic Design
Illustration
Industrial Design

Lettering and Calligraphy
Packaging Design
Perceptual Drawing
Publication Design
Reproduction
Three-dimensional Design
Two-dimensional Design
Typography
Visual Communication

OPTIONS WITHIN MAJOR

Exhibit Design
Graphic Design

Illustration

RECOMMENDED HIGH SCHOOL COURSES

Art
English

Graphics
Journalism

CAREERS	D.O.T. NUMBER	OUTLOOK	AVERAGE INITIAL SALARY
Associate Degree			
Graphic Artist	979.382-018	Good	$17,000
Bachelor Degrees			
Advertising Designer	247.387-010	Good	19,200
Commercial Artist	141.061-022	Fair	20,300
Commercial Designer	141.061-038	Good	21,200
Copy Artist	141.061-022	Fair	17,300
Fashion Artist	141.061-014	Good	21,200
Graphic Artist	979.382-018	Good	21,800
Illustrator	141.061-022	Good	19,300
Layout Designer	141.061-018	Good	19,000
Graduate Degree			
Professor	090.227-010	Good	32,900

Occupational Personality Styles: Artistic, Technical

DPT Functions: Data = H   People = L   Things = H

GOE Work Groups: Craft Arts, Promotion

Design Engineering Technology

The application of graphics technology to engineering design is an outgrowth of the space industry and has been spurred on by industrial needs and demands. Present graduates are qualified to work in various fields of engineering design, including consideration of new materials, technical graphics, computer-aided design, architectural design, automated graphics, aeronautical machine design, and special design courses in the strength of materials. Lucrative positions continue to be offered as the national demand for graduates continues to increase.

COURSE REQUIREMENTS

Applied Dynamics and Kinematics
Applied Mechanics
Applied Physics
Basic Computer-Assisted
  Part Programming
Basic Fluid Power
Computer-Aided Drafting
Descriptive Geometry
Design for Technology
Economy, Society, and
  Public Policy
Electrical Machines and
  Controls
Elements of Machines
Engineering Graphics
Manufacturing Processes
Materials Science—Nonmetals
Mechanical Drafting
Physical Metallurgy
Production Operations
Professional Graphic Application
Scientific Computing
Technical Mathematics
Technical Writing

OPTIONS WITHIN MAJOR

Architectural Design
Automated Graphics
Building Construction
Building Design
Computer-Aided Design
Computer Programming
Management in Design
Manufacturing Design
Production Design

RECOMMENDED HIGH SCHOOL COURSES

Chemistry
Drafting
Industrial Shop
Math (3 years)
Physics

CAREERS	D.O.T. NUMBER	OUTLOOK	AVERAGE INITIAL SALARY
Bachelor Degrees			
Architectural Drafter	001.261-010	Good	$18,100
Computer-Aided Designer	213.362-010	Excellent	24,500
Computer-Aided Drafter	005.281-010	Excellent	26,000
Design Engineer	007.061-018	Excellent	28,100
Engineering Assistant	007.061-018	Good/Exc.	18,100
Industrial Designer	142.061-026	Good	24,900
Industrial Engineer Technician	012.267-010	Good	18,900
Systems Programmer	030.162-022	Excellent	27,200
Graduate Degree			
Professor	090.227-010	Good	32,900

Occupational Personality Styles: Scientific, Technical

DPT Functions: Data = H   People = L   Things = H

GOE Work Groups: Engineering, Engineering Technology

Dietetics

Dietitians plan nutritious and appetizing meals to help people maintain or recover good health. They also supervise the food service personnel who prepare and serve the meals, manage dietetic purchasing and accounting, and give advice on good eating habits. Opportunities for employment are found in hospitals, nursing homes, clinics, colleges and universities, health-related agencies, restaurants, armed forces, and large companies that provide food service for their employees.

COURSE REQUIREMENTS

Bacteriology
Biochemistry
Chemistry
Clinical Nutrition
Community Nutrition
Data Processing
Dietetics
Economics
Food Analysis
Food and Nutrition
Food Chemistry

Human Anatomy
Human Physiology
Institution Management
Math
Medical Dietetics
Microbiology
Psychology
Sociology

OPTIONS WITHIN MAJOR

Foods and Nutrition
Institution Management

Research Dietitian

RECOMMENDED HIGH SCHOOL COURSES

Biology
Business Courses
Chemistry
Health

Home Economics
Math
Physiology
Psychology

CAREERS	D.O.T. NUMBER	OUTLOOK	AVERAGE INITIAL SALARY
Bachelor Degrees			
Clinical Dietitian	077.127-014	Good/Exc.	$20,000
Dietetic Educator	077.127-022	Good/Exc.	19,500
Nutritionist	096.121-014	Good/Exc.	19,000
Graduate Degrees			
Administrative Dietitian	077.117-010	Good/Exc.	28,000
Professor	090.227-010	Good/Exc.	32,900
Public Health Nutritionist	077.127-010	Good/Exc.	23,400
Research Dietitian	077.061-010	Good/Exc.	27,100

Occupational Personality Styles: Scientific, Social, Serving

DPT Functions: Data = H   People = H   Things = L

GOE Work Groups: Laboratory Technology, Life Sciences

Drafting

Drafting technicians assist engineers, architects, and designers with sketches, calculations, specifications, and materials needed on the job. Employment opportunities in industry, architects' offices, or government agencies involve use and knowledge of handbooks, tables, calculators, automated drafting machines, and traditional drafting equipment. The demand for drafters as supporting personnel to engineers and scientists, and as liaison between professional and nonprofessional people, will increase.

COURSE REQUIREMENTS

Commercial Structures
Computer-Aided Design
Computer-Assisted Drafting
Descriptive Geometry
Elements of Machines
Engineering Graphics
Graphics

Mechanical Drafting
   Perspective
Professional Graphics Application
Residential Drafting
Technical Math

OPTIONS WITHIN MAJOR

Architectural Drafting
Computer-Aided Technology

Mechanical Drafting

RECOMMENDED HIGH SCHOOL COURSES

Drafting
Math (3 years)

Physics

CAREERS	D.O.T. NUMBER	OUTLOOK	AVERAGE INITIAL SALARY
Associate Degrees			
Architectural Drafter	001.261-010	Fair	$16,000
Castings Drafter	007.261-014	Fair	16,000
Directional Drafter	010.281-010	Fair	16,000
Drafter	007.161-018	Good	17,600
Electrical Drafter	003.281-010	Fair/Good	17,600
Electronics Drafter	003.281-014	Fair/Good	17,600
Engineering Technician	007.161-126	Good	17,900
Patent Drafter	007.261-018	Good	21,000
Tool Design Drafter	007.261-022	Good	16,800
Bachelor Degrees			
Aeronautical Drafter	002.261-010	Good	25,200
Automotive Design Drafter	017.261-042	Good	21,900
Cartographic Drafter	018.261-010	Fair	20,000
Civil Drafter	005.281-010	Good	23,200
Design Drafter	017.261-014	Good/Exc.	26,200
Geological Drafter	010.281-014	Fair/Good	22,400
Geophysical Drafter	010.281-018	Fair/Good	22,400
Mechanical Drafter	007.281-010	Excellent	21,200
Structural Drafter	005.281-014	Excellent	21,200
Topographical Drafter	005.281-010	Fair	20,000

Occupational Personality Styles:	Scientific, Technical, Detail-oriented
DPT Functions:	Data = H People = L Things = H
GOE Work Group:	Engineering Technology

Early Childhood Education

Early childhood education combines a knowledge of basic developmental and behavioral characteristics of the child with appropriate teaching skills to prepare students to become preschool and elementary teachers, or effective parents. As the early stages of education set the future pattern for many students, well-qualified instructors are in demand despite the abundance of elementary teachers in many areas of the country. Although many students teach in public or private schools, a great number of graduates find training in early childhood education an asset in their home, community, and church life.

COURSE REQUIREMENTS

Art
Child Development
Child Psychology
Children's Literature
Geography
Math
Music for Elementary Teachers

Physical Education
Skill Analysis and Rhythm/Dance
School Health
Student Teaching
The Child in the Family
World Affairs

OPTIONS WITHIN MAJOR

Early Childhood Education
Elementary School

Kindergarten
Preschool

RECOMMENDED HIGH SCHOOL COURSES

Home Economics
Psychology

Sociology

CAREERS	D.O.T. NUMBER	OUTLOOK	AVERAGE INITIAL SALARY
Bachelor Degrees			
Day Care Center Worker	359.677-018	Good	$14,500
Elementary Teacher	092.227-010	Good	19,500
Kindergarten Teacher	092.227-014	Good	19,500
Nursery School Director	092.167-010	Good	20,200
Preschool Teacher	092.227-018	Good/Exc.	19,500
Graduate Degrees			
Counselor	045.107-010	Good	23,500
Professor	090.227-010	Good	32,900

Occupational Personality Styles: Serving, Social

DPT Functions: Data = H   People = H   Things = M

GOE Work Groups: Child and Adult Care, Educational and Library Services

Economics

The study of economics provides a broad view of national and international business conditions and an understanding of production, distribution, and consumption. It provides business people and government officials with vital information on matters such as prices, markets, domestic and foreign trade, and government policies. Students majoring in economics have considerable latitude in occupation selection. Graduates often pursue law school, graduate work in business (MBA), or economics, as well as going into business or government service.

COURSE REQUIREMENTS

Calculus
Econometrics
Economic Analysis of Decision
Economic, Society, and
   Public Policy
Math

Mathematical Statistics
Quantitative Methods
Statistics
Theory of Income
Theory of Price

OPTIONS WITHIN MAJOR

Applied Economics

Economic Theory

RECOMMENDED HIGH SCHOOL COURSES

Algebra
English

Trigonometry

CAREERS	D.O.T. NUMBER	OUTLOOK	AVERAGE INITIAL SALARY
Bachelor Degrees			
Market Research Analyst	050.067-014	Good/Exc.	$25,100
Stockbroker	250.257-018	Good/Exc.	34,000
Graduate Degrees			
Business Market Research Analyst	050.067-014	Good/Exc.	40,100
Economist	050.067-010	Good/Exc.	40,000
Government Economist	050.067-010	Good/Exc.	32,400
Professor	090.227-010	Good/Exc.	32,900

Occupational Personality Style: Scientific

DPT Functions: Data = H   People = L   Things = L

GOE Work Groups: Business Administration, Social Research

Educational Psychology

Educational psychology offers programs that prepare students to teach in special-education settings that deal with intellectual handicaps, behavior disorders, speech or auditory disabilities, and other communicative or learning problems. Certification is required for those desiring to teach in the public schools and can be incorporated with a regular four-year program. Owing to national legislation, which requires free, appropriate education for all handicapped children, the demand for special-education teachers, administrators, and personnel to provide training has increased significantly. To meet the needs of the handicapped and to fulfill these requirements, qualified graduates should be in demand for some time to come.

COURSE REQUIREMENTS

Audiology
Behavior Modifications
Behavior Problems
Communicative Disorders
Development and Learning
Exceptional Children
Group Counseling

Mental Retardation
Phonetics
School Guidance
School Psychology
Sign Language
Testing Techniques

OPTIONS WITHIN MAJOR

Counseling
Intellectually Handicapped
Learning Disabilities

School Psychology
Teaching Emotionally
  Handicapped

RECOMMENDED HIGH SCHOOL COURSES

English
Math
Psychology

Sociology
Speech

CAREERS	D.O.T. NUMBER	OUTLOOK	AVERAGE INITIAL SALARY
Bachelor Degrees			
Learning Specialist	094.227-022	Excellent	$19,500
Resource Teacher	094.227-030	Excellent	19,500
Special Education Teacher	094.227-030	Excellent	19,500
Teacher of the Mentally Retarded	094.227-030	Excellent	19,500
Therapist for the Blind	076.224-014	Fair	17,800
Graduate Degrees			
Career Assessment Officer	045.107-042	Good	22,000
Career Counselor	045.117-010	Good/Exc.	26,500
Counseling Psychologist	045.107-026	Good	31,700
Counselor	045.107-010	Good/Exc.	23,500
Director of Counseling	045.107-018	Fair/Good	35,400
Director of Guidance	045.117-010	Fair/Good	32,100
Educational Psychologist	045.067-010	Good	27,700
Mental Health Counselor	045.107-010	Fair	24,500
Professor	090.227-010	Good	32,900
School Counselor	045.107-010	Good	23,900
School Psychologist	045.107-034	Good	26,000
State Rehabilitation Counselor	045.107-042	Fair	21,000
Substance Abuse Counselor	045.107-058	Excellent	24,500

Occupational Personality Styles:	Scientific, Serving
DPT Functions:	Data = H People = H Things = L
GOE Work Groups:	Educational and Library Services, Social Research, Social Services

Electrical Engineering

Electrical engineers apply a thorough knowledge of electricity and education in physics, chemistry, and mathematics to develop systems and equipment used in the generation, transmittal, and reception of information and energy. Solid-state electronic devices must be designed for thousands of new applications each year. Current demands on resources for more electrical power, communications systems, and computer systems increase the need for electrical engineers. The need for thousands more in the field of electrical engineering and technical manpower requirements provide many opportunities.

COURSE REQUIREMENTS

Analytical Geometry/Calculus
Applied Ordinary Differential
  Equations
Beginning Mechanics—Static
Circuit Analysis
College Chemistry
Computer Engineering
Digital Computer Electronics
Electric Circuit Numerical
  Solutions
Electrical Circuits/Devices

Electrical Energy Conversion
Electrical Engineering
Elements of Thermoscience
Engineering Graphics
Engineering Mechanics—
  Dynamics
Feedback Concepts
Numerical Solutions in Electrical
  Engineering
Principles of Physics

OPTIONS WITHIN MAJOR

Computer Electronics
Electrical Power

Power
Solid-state Communications

RECOMMENDED HIGH SCHOOL COURSES

Algebra
Chemistry
Physics

Plane Geometry
Trigonometry

The Career Connection for College Education

CAREERS	D.O.T. NUMBER	OUTLOOK	AVERAGE INITIAL SALARY
Bachelor Degrees			
Applications Engineer	007.061-038	Good	$25,200
Communications Engr.	003.167-034	Good	24,900
Design Engineer	003.061-018	Excellent	28,400
Electrical Engineer	003.061-010	Fair/Good	30,900
Electrical Test Engineer	003.061-014	Fair/Good	29,000
Electronics Engineer	003.061-030	Good	31,600
Electronics Test Engr.	003.061-042	Good	33,100
Electro-optical Engineer	023.061-010	Good	27,800
Power, Solid-State Engr.	003.167-018	Excellent	32,100
Graduate Degrees			
Administration/Management Engineer		Good	40,100
Consulting Engineer		Good	42,000
Development and Research Engineer	003.061-026	Excellent	42,400
Engineering Professor	090.227-010	Excellent	32,900
Systems Engineer	003.167-026	Excellent	39,000

Occupational Personality Styles: Scientific, Technical

DPT Functions: Data = H   People = L   Things = H

GOE Work Group: Engineering Technology

Electronics Engineering Technology

Electronics engineering technologists apply electronic devices and systems to the control of equipment in industry, laboratories, and the home. Graduates are prepared to enter shipbuilding, medical electronics, research laboratories, aerospace industries, communication, computer productions, and a variety of industries on the basis of their knowledge of electronic circuit principles, equipment operations, and digital-computer hardware and software. Electronic technicians (with two-year degrees) are prepared to assist engineers with practical and detailed work in any of the industries listed above. Because of the rapid increase in digital-computer use in all walks of life, as well as other essential contributions of electronics, the occupational opportunities in this field are tremendous.

COURSE REQUIREMENTS

Analytical Geometry
Applied Physics
Audio Communications Systems
Calculus
Communications Circuits
Communications Systems
Computer-Aided Instrumentation
Computer Science
Control Systems
Data Transmission
DC and AC Circuits
Digital Circuits
Digital Electronics
Economics
Electrical Drawing
Electrical Troubleshooting

Electronic Fabrication
   and Assembly
Electronic Instrumentation
Electronical Control Systems
Electronics
High Frequency Systems
Industrial Electronics
Linear Integrated Circuits
Minicomputer Applications
Process Control Computers
Physics
Radio Broadcast Systems
Real-time Computer Systems
Technical Math
Technical Writing
TV Broadcast Systems

OPTIONS WITHIN MAJOR

Circuit Analysis
Communications
Computer-Aided Processes
Digital Electronics

Electronic Technology
Instrumentation
Minicomputer Applications

Electrical Shop   Physics
Math (3 years)

CAREERS	D.O.T. NUMBER	OUTLOOK	AVERAGE INITIAL SALARY
Associate Degrees			
Electrical Power Tech.	720.281-018	Good/Exc.	$19,000
Electronics Technician	003.161-014	Fair/Good	19,600
Bachelor Degrees			
Communications Engineer	003.167-034	Good	24,900
Communications Technologist	003.161-014	Excellent	25,100
Computer Designer		Excellent	27,400
Computer Technologist	033.167-010	Good/Exc.	29,000
Electronics Engineer	003.061-030	Good	31,600
Electronics System Mgr.	828.161-010	Fair	26,100
Electronics System Specialist	828.261-022	Good/Exc.	28,900
Electronics Test Engineer	003.061-014	Good	33,100
Television and Audio Systems Specialist	726.261-014	Excellent	24,300
Graduate Degree			
Professor	090.227-010	Good	32,900

Occupational Personality Styles: Scientific, Technical

DPT Functions: Data = H   People = L   Things = H

GOE Work Group: Engineering Technology

Elementary Education

Elementary-school teachers face the awesome challenge of teaching a diversity of subject matter to young minds in an effort to mold and prepare them for life's future challenges. A variety of experiences is to be had throughout the United States, but in some areas the supply of elementary teachers exceeds the demand. Despite the numbers available, there is still a great need for innovative, excellent elementary teachers.

COURSE REQUIREMENTS

Art for Elementary Grades
Basic Concepts of Math
Child Development
Educational Psychology
Elementary Music Methods
Geography

Instructional Methods
P.E.—Primary Grades
School Health
School Law
World Affairs

OPTIONS WITHIN MAJOR

Teaching

RECOMMENDED HIGH SCHOOL COURSES

Art
Biology
English (4 years)
History

Math
Music
Psychology
Science

CAREERS	D.O.T. NUMBER	OUTLOOK	AVERAGE INITIAL SALARY
Bachelor Degrees			
Audiovisual Specialist	100.167-010	Fair	$19,000
Teacher	091.227-010	Good/Exc.	19,500
Graduate Degrees			
Educational Administrator	099.117-026	Fair/Good	53,600
Principal	099.117-018	Fair	53,600

Occupational Personality Styles: Serving, Social

DPT Functions: Data = H   People = H   Things = L

GOE Work Group: Educational and Library Services

English

Although accurate usage of the English language is essential to the college graduate, encountering the humanizing forces of languages and literature is the primary objective of the English major. The graduate of English is prepared for numerous career possibilities, including teaching, business, law, or graduate school. The combined liberal arts and analytical and writing skill preparation is useful in most graduate studies as well as library science, communications, and journalism. The demand for English teachers still exceeds the supply of graduates each year, and other students are finding success in related fields.

COURSE REQUIREMENTS

American Literature	Folklore
Creative Writing	Grammar
Critical and Interpretive Writing	Novel
Drama	Science Fiction
English	Semantics
Exposition and Report Writing	Short Story

OPTIONS WITHIN MAJOR

Professional Writing	Teaching

RECOMMENDED HIGH SCHOOL COURSES

English	Literature
Foreign Language	Writing
Humanities	

CAREERS	D.O.T. NUMBER	OUTLOOK	AVERAGE INITIAL SALARY
Bachelor Degrees			
Book Editor	132.067-014	Fair	$26,500
Copywriter	131.067-014	Good	17,500
Editor	132.067-014	Good	25,200
Newspaper Editor	132.017-014	Fair	27,400
Poet	131.067-042	Poor/Fair	Varies
Proofreader	209.387-030	Fair/Good	15,300
Prose Writer	131.067-046	Good	Varies
Publications Editor	132.037-022	Good	25,200
Screenwriter	131.067-050	Good	29,700
Story Editor	132.037-026	Poor	20,400
Teacher	091.227-010	Good	19,500
Technical Scientific Editor	132.017-018	Good	26,800
Technical Writer	131.267-026	Good/Exc.	24,500
Graduate Degrees			
Critic	131.067-018	Fair	34,700
Professor	090.227-010	Good	32,900

Occupational Personality Styles:	Scientific, Social, Influencing
DPT Functions:	Data = H People = L Things = L
GOE Work Groups:	Communications, Educational and Library Services, Literary Arts

Environmental Health

Environmental health involves the application of science and education in the prevention of disease and injury. Environmentalists deal with the identification and correction of health problems involving water, soil, and air pollution, and waste and sewage disposal. They manage the quality of milk, food, and drugs, and the control of rodents, insects, and various other pests. They also work with radiation and noise hazards, effective housing and space utilization, sanitation of schools and institutions, and infection control in hospitals and other public facilities. Employment opportunities should remain positive with local, state, and federal departments of health; hospitals and health care operations; and in industry.

COURSE REQUIREMENTS

Basic Computers
Community Health
Environmental Health
Environmental Physics
Epidemiology
Fieldwork in Public Health
Food Microbiology
General Microbiology
Health of the Body Systems

Human Parasitology
Human Physiology
Leadership Development
Occupational/Industrial Health
Organic Chemistry
Safety Education
State/Local Government Policy
Statistics
Water/Sewage Microbiology

OPTIONS WITHIN MAJOR

Governmental Agencies

Industrial Staff

RECOMMENDED HIGH SCHOOL COURSES

Biology
Chemistry
Health

Math (3 years)
Physical Science

CAREERS	D.O.T. NUMBER	OUTLOOK	AVERAGE INITIAL SALARY
Bachelor Degrees			
Community Health Planner	079.167-010	Fair/Good	$19,500
Environmental Health Specialist	029.261-014	Good	18,000
Food and Drug Inspector	168.267-042	Fair	16,800
Food Technologist	041.081-010	Good	27,400
Health Care Inspector	168.167-042	Fair	18,100
Health and Safety Inspector	168.167-062	Fair	18,100
Industrial Hygienist	079.061-010	Fair	31,200
Pollution Control Officer	019.081-018	Good	17,100
Public Health Officer	187.117-050	Good	17,100
Public Health Worker	187.117-050	Fair	17,100
Quality Control Officer	168.167-062	Fair	17,300
Sanitation Officer	079.117-018	Fair	22,300
Graduate Degrees			
Environmental Health Scientist	029.081-010	Good	28,000
Professor	090.227-010	Fair	32,900

Occupational Personality Styles: Scientific, Social

DPT Functions: Data = H People = L Things = L

GOE Work Group: Medical Sciences

European Studies

European studies is an interdisciplinary program typically referred to as "area studies." It integrates ideas and principles from anthropology, literature, history, geography, and economics. This broadly based education allows one to do historical research, social, political, and economic analysis, and literary criticism. Students often continue on to advanced studies in law, business administration, or liberal arts, or may become involved in teaching or government service.

COURSE REQUIREMENTS

Arts in the Western Culture
Baroque Art
Comparative Economic Systems
Comparative Literature
Contemporary European Art
Cultural Geography
Economic Analysis
Economic History of Europe
English Literature
European Art and Architecture
European Geography
French Literature
Geography and World Affairs
German Literature

History of Musical Style
International Trade and Finance
Italian Art
Italian Literature
Nineteenth-Century Europe
Origins of Western Philosophy
Political Geography
Renaissance Art
Romantic Music
The Age of Enlightenment
The Reformation
The Renaissance
Twentieth-Century Europe
World Civilizations

OPTIONS WITHIN MAJOR

Business
Culture
Geography

Government
Philosophy

RECOMMENDED HIGH SCHOOL COURSES

Art
Economics
English
Foreign Language

Geography
History
Literature

The Career Connection for College Education

CAREERS	D.O.T. NUMBER	OUTLOOK	AVERAGE INITIAL SALARY
Bachelor Degrees			
Biographer	052.067-010	Fair/Poor	Varies
Correspondent	131.267-018	Fair	$24,000
Foreign-Service Officer	188.117-106	Fair	25,100
Historian	052.067-022	Fair/Poor	25,200
Import/Export Agent	184.117-022	Good	23,100
Intelligence Expert	059.267-010	Good	25,900
Public Relations Specialist	165.167-014	Fair	29,100
Publications Editor	132.037-022	Poor	20,300
Travel Agent	252.152-010	Good	17,200
Graduate Degrees			
Foreign Service	051.067-010	Good	30,200
Professor	090.227-010	Good	32,900
Researcher	199.267-034	Good	30,000

Occupational Personality Styles: Social, Scientific

DPT Functions: Data = H   People = M   Things = L

GOE Work Group: Social Research

Family Resource Management

Family resource management consists of training in the development of managerial skills directly related to financial security, consumer satisfaction, and successful family living. The practical skills and knowledge obtained serves the individual and opens employment opportunities in finance, education, social services, government, business, and any other area that requires consumer and family finance, home management, or household equipment specialization. Increasing possibilities are available with government agencies, educational institutions, financial firms, and private companies of all sorts. Various opportunities are also opening up in foreign nations to train and assist populations in basic management skills.

COURSE REQUIREMENTS

Consumer Behavior	Family Management
Consumer Law	Family Money Management
Economics of Consumption	Housing and Lighting
Family and Consumer	Housing Equipment
Economics	Residence Management
Family Estate Planning	Space Planning
Family Financial Analysis	

OPTIONS WITHIN MAJOR

Consumer Affairs	Family Financial Planning
Equipment, Foods, Housing	Family Management

RECOMMENDED HIGH SCHOOL COURSES

Economics	Psychology
Family Living	Sociology
Personal Finance	

CAREERS	D.O.T. NUMBER	OUTLOOK	AVERAGE INITIAL SALARY
Bachelor Degrees			
Consumer Affairs Staff	096.121-014	Fair	$19,200
Estate Planner	186.167-010	Excellent	31,400
Extension Service Specialist	096.127-014	Good	20,000
Family Financial Planning and Counseling	169.267-018	Good	25,500
Family/Social Services Staff	195.107-034	Fair	18,200
Graduate Degree			
Professor	090.227-010	Good	32,900

Occupational Personality Styles: Social, Influencing

DPT Functions: Data = H   People = H   Things = L

GOE Work Groups: Business Management, Finance

Finance and Banking

Commercial banks constitute one of the fastest growing industries in our economy. Because banks employ specialized techniques and equipment in very detailed work, most employees gain experience and skill through on-the-job training. Banks usually seek college graduates for officer trainee jobs. However, many openings exist for high school graduates in other bank positions. Bank employees generally have good opportunities for advancement.

COURSE REQUIREMENTS

Administrative Data Processing
Business in Urban Society
Business Statistics
Capital Budgeting
Finance Management
Industrial Operations
   Management
Introduction to Accounting

Investment Finance
Managerial Accounting
Managerial Economics
Money and Banking
Principles of Finance
Principles of Marketing

OPTIONS WITHIN MAJOR

Banking
Finance

Insurance

RECOMMENDED HIGH SCHOOL COURSES

Accounting
Bookkeeping
Business Machine Operation

Commercial Law
Computer Operation
Data Processing

CAREERS	D.O.T. NUMBER	OUTLOOK	AVERAGE INITIAL SALARY
Bachelor Degrees			
Assistant Vice-president	186.117-078	Good	$35,000
Broker	162.157-018	Good/Exc.	34,000
Chief Executive Officer or President	186.117-054	Good	52,900
Controller	160.167-058	Fair	25,800
Estate Planner	186.167-010	Excellent	31,400
Financial Aid Officer	090.117-030	Good	24,800
Financial Analyst	020.167-010	Good	24,800
Loan Officer	186.267-018	Good	24,800
Senior and Executive Vice-president	186.117-078	Good	42,000
Treasurer	161.117-018	Fair	28,600
Trust Officer	186.117-074	Good	26,300
Underwriter	169.267-046	Good	24,100

Occupational Personality Styles: Detail-oriented, Influencing

DPT Functions: Data = H   People = M   Things = L

GOE Work Groups: Business Management, Finance

Food Science

Food science deals with the application of biological, physical, and social sciences in solving world food and nutritional problems. A study of food production from raw food sources allows a student to prepare for professional vocations such as directing food quality, researching and developing new foods, managing food processing inspection, working in test kitchens, or serving as a medical dietitian. Nutritionists work in health-related services in the community, state, or nation and as consultants for private pharmaceutical or food industries. The food scientist deals more with the research, quality control, and inspection of products in the food industry.

COURSE REQUIREMENTS

Biochemistry	Food Processing
Chemistry	Food Production
Clinical Nutrition	Food Quality Preservation
College Algebra	Food Research/Development
Community Nutrition	Food Science
Dietetics	Human Anatomy
Experimental Human Nutrition	Human Nutrition
Experiments in Nutrition	Human Physiology
Family Money Management	Medical Dietetics
Food Analysis	Microbiology
Food Chemistry	Organization Behavior
Food Microbiology	Physics
Food Preservation	Quantitative/Qualitative Analysis

OPTIONS WITHIN MAJOR

Food Science	Medical Dietetics
Food Systems Administration	Nutrition

RECOMMENDED HIGH SCHOOL COURSES

Biology	English
Botany	Math
Business	Physics
Chemistry	

CAREERS	D.O.T. NUMBER	OUTLOOK	AVERAGE INITIAL SALARY
Bachelor Degrees			
Dietitian	077.117-010	Good/Exc.	$20,000
Food Chemist	041.081-010	Fair	23,600
Food Systems Mgt.	319.136-010	Good	21,900
Food Technologist	041.081-010	Good	27,000
Public Health Officer	187.117-050	Good	17,000
Quality Control Officer	168.167-062	Fair	17,300
Teacher	091.227-010	Fair	19,500
Test Kitchen Specialist		Fair	14,200
Graduate Degrees			
Food Scientist	041.081-010	Good	28,400
Professor	090.227-010	Good	32,900

Occupational Personality Styles: Scientific, Technical

DPT Functions: Data = H   People = L   Things = M

GOE Work Group: Life Sciences

Forestry

Foresters plan and supervise the growing, protection, and utilization of trees. They make maps of forest areas, estimate the amount of standing timber and future growth, and manage timber sales. Other duties may range from wildlife protection and watershed management to supervision of camps, parks, and grazing lands. They must deal constantly with land owners, loggers, forestry aides, and a wide variety of other people. Qualified foresters find job opportunities available with private industry, the Forest Service of the Department of Agriculture, state and local governments, colleges and universities, and consulting firms.

COURSE REQUIREMENTS

Arboriculture
Dendrology
Field Studies
Forest Ecology
Forest Economics
Forest Management
Forest Protection

Forestry
Forest Soils
Harvesting Systems
Quantitative Methods
Tree Pathology
Wood Properties

OPTIONS WITHIN MAJOR

Forestry
Recreation

Tree Nursery

RECOMMENDED HIGH SCHOOL COURSES

Chemistry
English Literature

Physics
Public Speaking

The Career Connection for College Education

CAREERS	D.O.T. NUMBER	OUTLOOK	AVERAGE INITIAL SALARY
Associate Degree			
Forestry Technician	452.364-010	Fair/Good	$15,100
Bachelor Degrees			
Forest Ecologist	040.061-030	Fair	19,200
Forest Ranger	040.067-010	Fair/Good	19,200
Graduate Degrees			
M.S. Degree Forester	040.167-010	Good/Exc.	25,100
Ph.D. Forester		Good/Exc.	30,000
Professor/Research	090.227-010	Fair	32,900

Occupational Personality Styles: Scientific, Technical

DPT Functions: Data = H   People = L   Things = H

GOE Work Groups: Life Sciences, Business Administration

French

Students majoring in French prepare in language, culture, and literature for international business, banking, trade, airlines, or related professions in French-speaking nations (France, Switzerland, Belgium, and Canada). Teaching positions are also available in some areas, and many graduate and professional studies (medicine, etc.) require students to learn a foreign language. Many firms, as well as government agencies, are looking for someone who can communicate and think independently in more than one language.

COURSE REQUIREMENTS

Composition	Grammar
Conversation	Literature
Cultural Civilization	Phonetics
French	Translation

OPTIONS WITHIN MAJOR

Business	Translation Interpretation
Education	

RECOMMENDED HIGH SCHOOL COURSES

French	Humanities
Geography	Literature
History	Social Science

CAREERS	D.O.T. NUMBER	OUTLOOK	AVERAGE INITIAL SALARY
Bachelor Degrees			
Customs Official	168.267-022	Fair	$16,500
Foreign-Service Officer	188.117-106	Fair	24,000
Import/Export Agent	184.117-022	Good	25,100
Intelligence Expert	059.267-010	Good	25,200
Interpreter	137.267-014	Good	23,100
Language Researcher	059.067-014	Fair	25,900
Public Relations Specialist	165.167-014	Fair	29,100
Scientific Writer	131.267-026	Fair	25,300
Teacher	091.227-010	Good	19,500
Translator	137.267-018	Good	23,200
Travel Agent	252.152-010	Good	17,200
Graduate Degrees			
Professor	090.227-010	Good	32,900
Scientific Linguist	059.067-014	Fair	30,000

Occupational Personality Styles: Scientific, Social

DPT Functions: Data = H   People = M   Things = L

GOE Work Groups: Business Administration, Business Management, Educational and Library Services, Security Services

Genealogy

An upsurge across the nation has increased genealogical interest and research, both on a private and on a professional basis. Genealogy deals with searching, locating, recording, and preserving records of persons and families living or deceased. Currently, training is offered in two-year programs for individual needs to train professionals. Although career opportunities are limited, a degree in genealogy can prepare students for advanced studies in related fields.

COURSE REQUIREMENTS

Genealogy

Geographical History

Geography

History

Paleography

Research Methods

OPTIONS WITHIN MAJOR

Family Research

Individual Research

Professional Genealogy

RECOMMENDED HIGH SCHOOL COURSES

English

Foreign Language

Social Studies

CAREERS	D.O.T. NUMBER	OUTLOOK	AVERAGE INITIAL SALARY
Associate Degrees			
Genealogy Research Specialist	052.067-018	Fair/Poor	$20,000
Librarian	100.127-014	Fair	20,300

Occupational Personality Styles: Detail-oriented, Serving

DPT Functions: Data = H   People = L   Things = L

GOE Work Group: Social Research

Geography

Geography is the science of spatial analysis concerned primarily with interpreting the occurrence, distribution, and interrelationships of the physical and cultural patterns which can be discerned. Employment is available in many areas of private business and industry, government agencies, and education as cartographers, geographic analysts, land officers, climatologists, intelligence specialists, economists, and teachers. Excellent employment opportunities exist in city and region planning, industrial location research, and teaching on several levels.

COURSE REQUIREMENTS

Air Photo Interpretation
Biogeography
Climatology
Earth Ecosystems
Economic Geography
Geographics
Geographic Field Techniques
Geography

Geography of Culture
Geomorphology
Hydrology
Land-Use Planning
Maps and Air Photos
Resource Management
Soils
World Vegetation

OPTIONS WITHIN MAJOR

Cartography
Geographic Planning

Teaching
Travel/Tourism

RECOMMENDED HIGH SCHOOL COURSES

Foreign Language
Geography

Natural Science
Social Studies

CAREERS	D.O.T. NUMBER	OUTLOOK	AVERAGE INITIAL SALARY
Associate Degrees			
Planning/Cartographic Technician	018.261-026	Good	$18,100
Travel Agent	252.152-010	Fair	17,200
Bachelor Degrees			
Cartographer	018.261-026	Good	22,600
Climatologist		Good	20,100
Industrial Location Geographer	029.067-010	Good	22,000
Map Curator	102.017-010	Fair/Good	24,100
Teacher	091.227-010	Good	19,500
Travel Agent	252.152-010	Good	17,200
Urban Region Planner	199.167-014	Good	24,300
Graduate Degrees			
Environmental Researcher	003.261-010	Good	26,000
Geographer	029.067-010	Good	28,100
Physical Geographer	029.067-014	Good	28,100
Professor	090.227-010	Good	32,900

Occupational Personality Styles: Scientific, Technical

DPT Functions: Data = H   People = L   Things = L

GOE Work Group: Social Research

Geology

Geology involves the study of a wide variety of topics dealing with earth and life sciences. Geologists use a spectrum of knowledge from physics, chemistry, mathematics, botany, zoology, and related fields. They deal with energy, mineral research and discovery, environmental geology, oceanography, and other outdoor field studies or indoor laboratory investigations. Engineering geologists apply geological principles to a variety of projects including highways, dams, reservoirs, tunnels, pipelines, subdivisions, power plants, land-use planning, and related areas. Students of geology who tend toward earth science can prepare for a composite science teaching career on the secondary level. Job opportunities are available in industry, academic areas, and government agencies throughout the world.

COURSE REQUIREMENTS

Algebra	Marine Geology
Analytical Geometry	Mineralogy
Astrogeology	Optical Mineralogy
Calculus	Organic Chemistry
Chemistry	Paleontology
Earth Processes	Petrology
Economic Geology	Physical Geology
Geological Literature	Principles of Physics
Geological Methods	Sedimentation
Geomorphology	Stratigraphy
Historical Geology	Structural Geology
Inorganic Chemistry	Trigonometry

OPTIONS WITHIN MAJOR

Earth Science	Geology
Engineer Geology	

RECOMMENDED HIGH SCHOOL COURSES

Chemistry	Math (3 years)
Computer Science	Physics

CAREERS	D.O.T. NUMBER	OUTLOOK	AVERAGE INITIAL SALARY
Bachelor Degrees			
Geodesist	024.061-014	Good	$22,700
Geologist	024.061-018	Excellent	22,700
Groundwater Engineer		Good	25,100
Hydrologist	024.061-034	Fair	22,300
Land-Use Planner	199.167-014	Good	23,400
Mineralogist	024.061-038	Good/Exc.	23,600
Mining Geologist/Engineer	024.061-018	Excellent	32,900
Seismologist	024.061-050	Good	25,500
Stratigrapher	024.061-057	Fair/Good	22,300
Teacher	091.227-010	Good	19,500
Graduate Degrees			
Geophysicist	024.061-030	Excellent	31,600
Paleontologist	024.062-042	Good	30,400
Petroleum Geologist	024.061-022	Excellent	31,000
Petroleum Geologist Engineer	024.061-022	Excellent	35,000
Petrologist	024.061-046	Good	29,800
Professor	090.227-010	Good	32,900
Research	024.061-030	Good	33,400

Occupational Personality Styles:	Scientific, Technical
DPT Functions:	Data = H People = L Things = H
GOE Work Group:	Physical Sciences

Geophysics

Geophysicists study the composition and physical aspects of the earth and its electric, magnetic, and gravitational fields. They often use satellites to conduct tests from outer space and computers to collect and analyze data. Geophysicists usually specialize in one of three general phases of the science—solid earth, fluid earth, or upper atmosphere. Some may also study other planets.

Most geophysicists work in private industry, chiefly for petroleum or natural gas companies. Others are in mining companies, exploration and consulting firms, and research institutes. A few are independent consultants and some do geophysical prospecting on a fee or contract basis. Many geophysicists and hydrologists work for federal government agencies, mainly the U.S. Geological Survey, the National Oceanic and Atmospheric Administration, and the Defense Department. Other geophysicists work for colleges and universities, state governments, and nonprofit research institutions.

COURSE REQUIREMENTS

Chemistry	Geophysics
Climates	Gravity Fields
Experimental Geology	Instrumentation
Experimental Petrology	Isotope Geochemistry
Exploration Geophysics	Magnetic Fields
Geographics	Minerals
Geomorphology	Physics
Geophysical Exploration	Seismic Waves

OPTIONS WITHIN MAJOR

Industrial Geophysics	Teaching
Research	

RECOMMENDED HIGH SCHOOL COURSES

Chemistry	Math
Earth Science	Physics
Geology	

The Career Connection for College Education

CAREERS	D.O.T. NUMBER	OUTLOOK	AVERAGE INITIAL SALARY
Bachelor Degrees			
Geodesist	024.061-014	Good	$22,700
Hydrologist	024.061-034	Fair	22,300
Seismologist	024.061-050	Good	25,500
Stratigrapher	024.061-057	Fair/Good	22,300
Graduate Degrees			
Geophysicist	024.061-030	Excellent	31,600
Paleomagnetician	024.061-042	Excellent	30,400
Paleontologist	024.061-062	Good	30,400
Professor	090.227-010	Good	32,900

Occupational Personality Style: Scientific

DPT Functions: Data = H   People = L   Things = L

GOE Work Group: Physical Sciences

German

A study of German provides the student with a broad liberal arts background for specialized graduate study or teaching at the secondary level. Because of the shortage of teaching positions, many language majors are turning to law, medicine, or international business and law. Many industrial firms and government agencies are seeking graduates who are proficient in a second language and have an understanding of another culture.

COURSE REQUIREMENTS

Composition   Grammar
Conversation   Literature
Cultural Civilization   Phonetics
German   Translation

OPTIONS WITHIN MAJOR

Business   Interpretation
Education   Translation

RECOMMENDED HIGH SCHOOL COURSES

Geography   Humanities
German   Literature
History   Social Science

CAREERS	D.O.T. NUMBER	OUTLOOK	AVERAGE INITIAL SALARY
Bachelor Degrees			
Customs Official	168.267-022	Fair	$16,500
Foreign-Service Officer	188.117-106	Fair	24,000
Import/Export Agent	184.117-022	Good	25,100
Intelligence Expert	059.267-010	Good	25,200
Interpreter	137.267-014	Fair/Good	21,100
Language Researcher	059.067-014	Fair	25,900
Public Relations Specialist	165.167-014	Fair	29,100
Scientific Writer	131.267-026	Fair	25,300
Teacher	091.227-010	Good	19,500
Translator	137.267-018	Good	20,000
Travel Agent	252.152-010	Good	17,200
Graduate Degrees			
Professor	090.227-010	Good	32,900
Scientific Linguist	059.067-014	Fair	30,000

Occupational Personality Styles: Scientific, Social

DPT Functions: Data = H   People = M   Things = L

GOE Work Groups: Business Administration, Business Management, Educational and Library Services, Security Services

Health Administration

Administrators in health care work with medical doctors, nurses, and other professionals. In addition, they are responsible for proper care of the patients. The needs of the health institution are another responsibility of the administrator. A variety of facilities offer extended care, short-term care, emergency, same-day service, or a combination of some or all of these. Health care is undergoing dramatic changes. Dynamic and diversified management is needed to provide the leadership required in new and pioneering efforts.

COURSE REQUIREMENTS

Computers for Managers
Cooperative Education
Ethics
Financial Accounting
Financial Management
Health Financial Management
Health Service Economics
Health Service Organizations
Labor Relations
Legal Concepts
Marketing and Planning

Marketing Health Services
Medical Care
Operations Management
Oral Communications
Organizational Development
Personnel Management
Quantitative Analysis
Risk Analysis
Strategic Planning
Written Communication

OPTIONS WITHIN MAJOR

Clinic Administration

Hospital Administration

RECOMMENDED HIGH SCHOOL COURSES

Algebra

English

CAREERS	D.O.T. NUMBER	OUTLOOK	AVERAGE INITIAL SALARY
Graduate Degrees			
Hospital Administrator	187.117-010	Excellent	$38,900
Medical Facilities Director	188.117-082	Excellent	37,400
Professor	090.227-010	Excellent	32,900

Occupational Personality Styles: Influencing, Social

DPT Functions: Data = H   People = H   Things = L

GOE Work Groups: Business Administration, Medical Sciences

Health Science

Personal and public health are of major importance today, and educating young people about proper health and health problems is challenging and rewarding. Medical costs, drug abuse, venereal disease, quackery, and a multitude of health-related concerns provide a vast amount of information to be taught in the public schools. Accident prevention and treatment, as well as dealing with many of the problems of today's youth, provide challenges and make health education an interesting field.

COURSE REQUIREMENTS

Advanced First Aid
  Instructorship
Consumer Health
Drug Use and Abuse
Elementary Human Anatomy
Elementary Human Physiology
Essentials of Nutrition
Health Education
Health Service Teaching
  Methods

Human Heredity
Human Nutrition
Human Sexuality
Microbiology
Personal Health
Psychology of Adolescence
Safety Education
School Health/Community

OPTIONS WITHIN MAJOR

Education

Governmental Agencies

RECOMMENDED HIGH SCHOOL COURSES

Biology
Chemistry

Math

CAREERS	D.O.T. NUMBER	OUTLOOK	AVERAGE INITIAL SALARY
Bachelor Degrees			
Health Care Officer	168.167-018	Good	$22,000
Health Services Adviser	187.117-050	Good/Exc.	19,500
Health Teacher	091.227-010	Good	19,500
Industrial Hygienist	079.161-010	Fair	31,200
Public Health Educator	079.117-014	Fair	19,500
Sanitarian	079.117-018	Fair	22,300
Technical Writer	131.267-026	Good/Exc.	24,500
Graduate Degrees			
Health Scientist	015.021-010	Excellent	32,400
Human Performance Researcher		Good	38,600
Professor	090.227-010	Good/Exc.	32,900
Sports Psychologist		Good	34,600

Occupational Personality Styles: Scientific, Social, Serving

DPT Functions: Data = H   People = M   Things = L

GOE Work Groups: Educational and Library Services, Medical Sciences

History

History is the study of past civilizations and problems used to promote insight and understanding of the problems of today, preserve our great cultural heritage, and enrich our appreciation of man and his world. History broadens our perspective and allows us to discover the essential elements of human existence. As such, history prepares students for careers in teaching, law, business, government service, advertising, historical editing, and related areas. The surplus of qualified history teachers has limited opportunities in education, but graduates find placement in other occupations.

COURSE REQUIREMENTS

Diplomatic History
Geographical History
Great Historians
Historical Problems
History
Ideas and Man in Modern World
Main Issues in American History

Paleography
The American Heritage
Topics in History
United States History
Writing History
World Civilization

OPTIONS WITHIN MAJOR

Governmental Agencies
Preparation for Professional
  School

Teaching

RECOMMENDED HIGH SCHOOL COURSES

English (4 years)
Foreign Language

History

CAREERS	D.O.T. NUMBER	OUTLOOK	AVERAGE INITIAL SALARY
Bachelor Degrees			
Archivist	101.167-010	Fair	$25,100
Biographer	052.067-010	Fair/Poor	Varies
Editor/Journalist	132.067-014	Fair/Good	29,300
Foreign-Service Officer	188.117-106	Fair	24,000
Genealogist	052.067-018	Fair/Poor	20,000
Historian	052.067-022	Fair/Poor	25,200
Librarian	100.127-014	Poor	24,400
Supervisor of Historic Sites	052.067-022	Fair/Poor	20,000
Teacher	091.227-010	Poor	19,500
Graduate Degrees			
Historian	052.067-022	Good	28,800
Historical Society Director	052.067-014	Fair	34,300
Professor	090.227-010	Fair	32,900
Researcher	199.267-034	Good	25,000

Occupational Personality Styles: Scientific, Serving

DPT Functions: Data = H   People = L   Things = L

GOE Work Groups: Communications, Literary Arts, Social Research

Home Economics Education

Home economics education prepares students for professional roles in public schools, cooperative extension services, business, or industry. Knowledge and skills obtained in a broad family-living program are used to educate individuals and families for better family life, improving goods and services used by families, conducting research, and furthering favorable conditions for optimal family living. The integrated program deals with child development, family finances, economic management, nutritional needs, and interior design and furnishing. Jobs are plentiful and qualified instructors of resource management and homemaking skills easily find employment.

COURSE REQUIREMENTS

Child Development
Curriculum Development
Dress/Pattern Construction
Experiences with Children
Food Science
Home Economics Education
Home Management
Home Nursing
Household Equipment

Human Nutrition
Interior Design
Occupational Home Economics
    Education
Psychology of Clothing
Residence Management
Textiles
Textiles for Consumers
The Child in the Family

OPTIONS WITHIN MAJOR

Public Health Specialists

Teaching

RECOMMENDED HIGH SCHOOL COURSES

Art
Biology
Chemistry

English
Homemaking
Speech

CAREERS	D.O.T. NUMBER	OUTLOOK	AVERAGE INITIAL SALARY
Bachelor Degrees			
Extension Service Specialist	096.127-014	Good	$20,000
Home Economics Teacher	091.227-010	Fair	19,500
Home Economist	096.121-014	Fair	21,200
Graduate Degree			
Professor	090.227-010	Fair	32,900

Occupational Personality Styles:	Serving, Social
DPT Functions:	Data = H People = H Things = M
GOE Work Group:	Educational and Library Services

Horticulture

Horticulture is the science of growing fruits, vegetables, flowers, and ornamental plants. The concerns of the horticulturist range from improving the living environment to plant, fruit, and vegetable use and production. Greenhouse and nursery management, landscape design, and other areas of landscaping provide major employment opportunities.

COURSE REQUIREMENTS

Botany
Chemistry
College Algebra
Commercial Fruit Tree
    Production
Floral Design
Greenhouse Management
Home Landscape and Design
Horticultural Science
Irrigated Soils
Math

Nursery Science
Pest Management
Plant Biology
Plant Growth and Reproduction
Small Fruit Science
Soil Fertility
Soil Science
Turf Science
Weed Science

OPTIONS WITHIN MAJOR

Agribusiness
Production

Professional School Preparation

RECOMMENDED HIGH SCHOOL COURSES

Botany
Business
Chemistry

English
Math
Vocational Education

CAREERS	D.O.T. NUMBER	OUTLOOK	AVERAGE INITIAL SALARY
Associate Degrees			
Florist	142.081-010	Good	$14,000
Orchard Grower	403.161-010	Fair	Varies
Bachelor Degrees			
Editor/Writer, Garden Magazine	132.067-022	Fair	25,200
Editorial Writer	131.067-022	Fair	25,200
Horticulturist	040.061-038	Fair/Good	20,500
Landscape Architect	001.061-018	Fair/Good	20,100
Landscape Contractor/ Estimator	182.167-014	Good	17,000
Plant Breeder/Inspector	041.061-082	Fair	20,900
Soil Conservationist	040.061-054	Good	19,300
Graduate Degrees			
Plant Pathologist	041.061-086	Good	29,300
Professor	090.227-010	Fair	32,900
Research Horticulturist	040.061-038	Fair	29,300

Occupational Personality Styles: Technical, Artistic

DPT Functions: Data = M   People = L   Things = H

GOE Work Groups: Life Sciences, Managerial Work: Plants and Animals

Hotel Management

Hotel managers are responsible for operating their establishments profitably and satisfying guests. They determine room rates and credit policy, direct the operation of the food service, and manage the housekeeping, accounting, security, and maintenance departments of the hotel. Handling problems and coping with the unexpected are important parts of the job.

Most hotels promote employees who have proven their ability, usually as front-office clerks, to assistant managers and eventually to general managers. Employers are, however, increasingly emphasizing college education. A bachelor's degree in hotel and restaurant administration provides particularly strong preparation for a career in hotel management.

COURSE REQUIREMENTS

Accounting
Business Administration
Catering
Data Processing
Economics

Food Service Management
Hotel Administration
Hotel Maintenance Engineering
Housekeeping
Tourism

RECOMMENDED HIGH SCHOOL COURSES

Business
English
Foreign Language

Psychology
Public Speaking
Social Studies

CAREERS	D.O.T. NUMBER	OUTLOOK	AVERAGE INITIAL SALARY
Associate Degrees			
Hotel/Motel Clerk	238.368-038	Good	$14,000
Hotel Recreation Manager	187.167-122	Fair	16,800
Bachelor Degrees			
Food Services Director	319.136-010	Good	22,900
Hotel and Restaurant Administrator	187.117-038	Good	25,300

Occupational Personality Styles: Influencing, Social

DPT Functions: Data = H   People = M   Things = L

GOE Work Groups: Business Management, Hospitality Services

Industrial Administration

Physical plant administrators serve in supervisory positions in industry and in the physical plants of school districts, colleges, and universities. Plant Administration involves planning and directing construction of facilities as well as administering maintenance and operations programs once the plant is complete. Expansion in universities and colleges in addition to the many needs of private industry will provide several opportunities in physical plant administration.

COURSE REQUIREMENTS

Building Construction
Chemistry
Economics
Economy, Society, and
    Public Policy
Elementary Surveying
Engineering Graphics
Field Botany

Fundamental Accounting Policy
Industrial Safety
Manufacturing Processes
Organizational Behavior
Statistics
Technical Math
Undergraduate Seminar

OPTIONS WITHIN MAJOR

Physical Plant Administration

RECOMMENDED HIGH SCHOOL COURSES

Chemistry
Machine Shop

Math (3 years)
Physics

CAREERS	D.O.T. NUMBER	OUTLOOK	AVERAGE INITIAL SALARY
Bachelor Degrees			
Building Construction Supervisor	381.137-010	Good	$24,900
Construction Inspector	182.267-010	Fair	21,000
Field Supervisor		Good	21,000
Physical Facilities Planner	184.167-210	Fair	21,500
Physical Plant Administrator/Supervisor	189.117-022	Good	28,500
Plant Engineer	007.167-014	Good	27,800

Occupational Personality Styles: Technical, Influencing

DPT Functions: Data = H   People = M   Things = H

GOE Work Groups: Managerial Work: Mechanical, Quality Control, Systems Operation

Industrial Education

Industrial education prepares graduates for teaching technical or vocational education or industrial arts. An increased emphasis on vocational education and technical skills in various school programs has led to greater opportunities for industrial education teachers. Industrial education teachers who have a broad background in automotives, electronics, graphic arts, metals, plastics, and woods will have no problem locating a teaching position in a secondary school or a technical college.

COURSE REQUIREMENTS

Adult Industrial Education
Automotive Engines
Career Information/Guidance
Construction Practices
Electricity
Engineering Graphics
Fuel and Electrical Systems
Graphic Arts
Manufacturing
Metalwork Fundamentals

Plastics Processes
Power Sources of Industry
Power Tune-Up
Screen Processing
Sheet Metal
Shop Maintenance
Shop Management
Shop Planning
Woodwork Fundamentals

OPTIONS WITHIN MAJOR

Industrial Design

Industrial Education

RECOMMENDED HIGH SCHOOL COURSES

Automotive Shop
Drafting
Electricity

Graphic Arts
Metalwork
Woodwork

CAREERS	D.O.T. NUMBER	OUTLOOK	AVERAGE INITIAL SALARY
Bachelor Degrees			
Industrial Arts Teacher	091.221-010	Good	$19,500
Manual Arts Therapist	076.124-010	Fair	23,100
Technical Teacher	090.227-010	Good	19,500
Vocational Educator	091.221-010	Good	19,500
Graduate Degrees			
Administrator	097.167-010	Fair/Good	26,500
Coordinator	099.117-026	Fair/Good	23,000
Professor	090.227-010	Fair/Good	32,900

Occupational Personality Styles: Technical, Serving

DPT Functions: Data = H   People = M   Things = H

GOE Work Groups: Crafts, Craft Technology, Educational and Library Services

Information Management

Many colleges and universities have broadened typical secretarial technology programs to include business education and to take advantage of new computer technologies. In addition to preparation for secretarial opportunities, there is an emphasis on management and office supervision. Job settings are numerous and in a variety of industrial, educational, and business enterprises.

COURSE REQUIREMENTS

Accounting
Analytical Officer Operations
Business Correspondence
Business Education
Business Machines
Cooperative Business Education
Data Base Information
Economy, Society, and
    Public Policy
Ergonomics
General College Math
Information Systems
    Management

Microcomputer Programming
Office Administration
Office Automation
Principles of Statistics
Production Typing
Records Management
Shorthand
Stenographic Procedure
Systems Analysis
Transcription
Typing

OPTIONS WITHIN MAJOR

Data Processing
Office Management

Shorthand
Typing

RECOMMENDED HIGH SCHOOL COURSES

Business
Business Machines
English

Math (3 years)
Shorthand
Typing

CAREERS	D.O.T. NUMBER	OUTLOOK	AVERAGE INITIAL SALARY
Associate Degrees			
Administrative Assistant	169.167-010	Excellent	$20,000
Clerk-Typist	203.362-010	Good	14,300
Data Typist	203.582-054	Good	15,900
Executive Secretary	189.117-010	Excellent	21,000
Legal Secretary	201.362-010	Excellent	16,500
Medical Secretary	201.362-014	Good	16,000
Receptionist	237.367-038	Good	14,400
School Secretary	201.362-022	Poor	15,600
Secretary	201.362-030	Excellent	18,600
Stenographer	202.362-014	Fair	16,100
Terminal Operator	213.362-010	Excellent	14,300
Transcribing Machine Operator	203.582-058	Fair	14,300
Typist	203.582-066	Excellent	14,300
Word Processing Supervisor	203.137-010	Excellent	22,900

Occupational Personality Styles: Detail-oriented, Influencing, Social

DPT Functions: Data = H   People = L   Things = H

GOE Work Groups: Administrative Detail, Clerical Machine Operation, Clerical Handling, Contracts and Claims, Mathematical Detail, Oral Communications

Insurance

The insurance industry offers many employment opportunities for both recent high school and college graduates and experienced workers. About one-half of all insurance employees work in life insurance companies and agencies. Employment of insurance workers is expected to increase about as fast as average for all occupations through the 1990s as the insurance industry continues to expand.

COURSE REQUIREMENTS

Comparative Public Financial Security
Employee Benefit Plans
Employee Medical Care
Estate Planning
Financial Security Program
Financing Medical Care
Life and Disability Insurance

Life and Health Insurer Operation
Personal Income Maintenance
Personal Insurance Planning
Problems in Risk and Insurance
Property and Liability Insurance
Property and Liability Operation
Risk Management Insurance

OPTIONS WITHIN MAJOR

Commercial Insurance
Estate Planning

Personal Insurance

RECOMMENDED HIGH SCHOOL COURSES

Biology
Business Law
Math

Public Speaking
Typing

CAREERS	D.O.T. NUMBER	OUTLOOK	AVERAGE INITIAL SALARY
Bachelor Degrees			
Actuary	020.167-010	Good/Exc.	$27,500
Claims Adjuster	241.217-010	Fair/Good	20,000
Claims Examiner	241.267-018	Fair/Good	22,000
Insurance Underwriter	250.257-010	Excellent	21,500
Sales Agent	251.357-010	Excellent	23,600

Occupational Personality Styles:	Influencing, Social
DPT Functions:	Data = H People = M Things = L
GOE Work Groups:	Business Management, Contracts and Claims, General Sales

Japanese

With increased importance in international commerce, Japan has become a leader in world trade, and students of Japanese find tremendous opportunities in international business and law. Besides business, Japanese is a key language in research in many graduate fields and in the significant study of world history and Asian studies. Five avenues of employment make up the bulk of opportunities for the graduate—government service, business, language research, teaching, and library sciences. Students of Japanese should supplement their language study with geography, comparative literature, and related fields.

COURSE REQUIREMENTS

Composition
Conversation
Grammar
Japanese

Literature
Phonetics
Translation

OPTIONS WITHIN MAJOR

Business
Education

Translation/Interpretation

RECOMMENDED HIGH SCHOOL COURSES

Foreign Language
Geography
History

Humanities
Literature
Social Science

CAREERS	D.O.T. NUMBER	OUTLOOK	AVERAGE INITIAL SALARY
Bachelor Degrees			
Customs Official	168.267-022	Fair	$16,500
Foreign-Service Officer	188.117-106	Fair	24,000
Import/Export Agent	184.117-022	Good	25,100
Intelligence Expert	059.267-010	Good	25,200
Interpreter	137.267-014	Fair/Good	20,000
Language Researcher	059.067-014	Fair	23,100
Public Relations Specialist	165.162-014	Fair/Good	29,100
Scientific Writer	131.267-026	Fair	25,300
Teacher	091.227-010	Poor	19,500
Translator	137.267-018	Good	20,000
Travel Agent	252.152-010	Good	17,200
Graduate Degrees			
Professor	090.227-010	Good	32,900
Scientific Linguist	059.067-014	Fair	30,000

Occupational Personality Styles: Scientific, Social

DPT Functions: Data = H   People = M   Things = L

GOE Work Groups: Business Administration, Business Management, Educational and Library Services, Security Services

Journalism

Journalism is the profession concerned with gathering, preparing, and communicating information to be presented through newspapers, magazines, trade publications, radio, television, news services, and other types of media. The work performed by journalists includes reporting, writing, editing, photographing, or broadcasting news items.

COURSE REQUIREMENTS

Advertising
Contemporary Journalism
Feature Writing
History of American Journalism
Industrial Publishing
Mass Communications
Mass Media
Newspaper Editing and Layout
Newswriting

Photojournalism
Public Affairs Reporting
Public Opinion
Public Relations
Radio News
Television News Film
The Law of Mass Media
Typography and Graphic Arts

OPTIONS WITHIN MAJOR

Journalism

Radio/Technician

RECOMMENDED HIGH SCHOOL COURSES

Composition
English Grammar
History

Literature
Math
Public Speaking

CAREERS	D.O.T. NUMBER	OUTLOOK	AVERAGE INITIAL SALARY
Bachelor Degrees			
Columnist	131.067-010	Fair	$21,000
Correspondent	131.267-018	Fair	24,000
Department Editor	132.037-018	Fair	21,000
Journalist	131.067-010	Fair	21,000
Managing Editor	132.017-010	Fair	Varies
News Analyst	131.067-010	Fair	27,800
News Editor	132.067-026	Fair	20,600
Newspaper Editor	132.017-014	Fair	27,400
Radio Newscaster	131.262-010	Fair	18,600
Reporter	131.262-018	Fair/Good	20,900
TV News Broadcaster	131.262-010	Fair	21,500
Graduate Degree			
Professor	090.227-010	Fair	32,900

Occupational Personality Styles: Influencing, Social, Scientific

DPT Functions: Data = H   People = M   Things = L

GOE Work Groups: Communications, Literary Arts

Landscape Architecture

Landscape architects are hired by many types of organizations, from real-estate firms starting new developments to municipalities constructing airports or parks. They usually plan the arrangement of vegetation, walkways, and other natural features of open spaces. They may also design areas where constructed materials predominate, as on streets that have been modified to improve pedestrian access and limit automobile traffic. They sometimes supervise the construction stages of outdoor projects.

COURSE REQUIREMENTS

Botany
City Planning
Design Communication
English
Greenhouse Management
Horticulture
Landscape Construction

Math
Nursery Science
Ornamental Horticulture
Science
Sketching
Soil-Plant Relationships
Surveying

RECOMMENDED HIGH SCHOOL COURSES

Art
Botany
English
Graphics

Math (2–3 years)
Mechanical Drawing
Public Speaking

CAREERS	D.O.T. NUMBER	OUTLOOK	AVERAGE INITIAL SALARY
Bachelor Degrees			
Environmental Designer	001.061-018	Fair	$18,900
Landscape Architect	001.061-018	Fair/Good	20,100
Landscape Contractor	182.167-014	Good	18,800

Occupational Personality Styles: Technical, Artistic

DPT Functions: Data = H   People = M   Things = H

GOE Work Groups: Life Sciences, Managerial Work: Plants and Animals

Latin American Studies

Latin American studies is an interdisciplinary program typically referred to as "area studies." It integrates ideas and principles from anthropology, literature, history, geography, and economics. This broadly based education allows one to do historical research, social, political, and economic analysis, and literary criticism. Students often continue on to advanced studies in law, business administration, or liberal arts, or may become involved in teaching or government service.

COURSE REQUIREMENTS

Archaeology of South America
Business and Culture
Central American Society
Colonization of Latin America
Comparative Governments
Economic Development
History of Argentina
History of Brazil
History of Chile

History of Mexico
Inter-American Relations
International Relations
Latin American Geography
Latin American Politics
Mesoamerican Archaeology
Mesoamerican History
Social Anthropology
Social Change in Latin America

OPTIONS WITHIN MAJOR

Archaeology/Anthropology
Business
Humanities

International Politics
Politics

RECOMMENDED HIGH SCHOOL COURSES

Art
Economics
English
Foreign Language

Geography
History
Literature

CAREERS	D.O.T. NUMBER	OUTLOOK	AVERAGE INITIAL SALARY
Bachelor Degrees			
Biographer	052.067-010	Fair/Poor	Varies
Correspondent	131.267-018	Fair	$24,000
Foreign-Service Officer	188.117-106	Fair	25,100
Historian	052.067-022	Fair/Poor	25,700
Import/Export Agent	184.117-022	Good	23,100
Intelligence Expert	059.267-010	Good	28,500
Public Relations Specialist	165.167-014	Fair	29,100
Publications Editor	132.037-022	Poor	25,300
Travel Agent	252.152-010	Good	17,200
Graduate Degrees			
Foreign Service	051.067-010	Good	30,100
Professor	090.227-010	Good	32,900
Researcher	199.267-037	Good	30,000

Occupational Personality Styles: Social, Scientific

DPT Functions: Data = H People = M Things = L

GOE Work Group: Social Research

Law

Every major industry, institution, and organization, as well as every individual citizen, is affected by the law to some degree. As a result, lawyers enter many careers and occupational opportunities. Approximately three-fourths of all the lawyers in the United States are in private practice, and the government employs the greatest number of salaried attorneys. A background in law also allows graduates opportunities in business (especially insurance firms), education, and politics. Although competition to enter law school is keen, the job market is wide open for those who complete the program.

COURSE REQUIREMENTS

General courses are emphasized on the bachelor degree or pre-law level with the following suggested areas:

English	Political Science
History	Psychology
Humanities	Speech

Graduate studies cover many aspects of law, including:

Accounting	Negotiations
Anti-trust	Oil and Gas
Civil Procedure	Public Land
Criminal	Regulative
Industries	Securities
Jurisprudence	State and Local Government
Labor	Trade Regulations
Legislation	Wills and Estates

RECOMMENDED HIGH SCHOOL COURSES

English	Math
History	Writing

CAREERS	D.O.T. NUMBER	OUTLOOK	AVERAGE INITIAL SALARY
Graduate Degrees			
Bar Examiner	110.167-010	Fair/Good	$39,900
Business Consultant	189.167-010	Excellent	Varies
Corporate Lawyer	110.117-022	Excellent	38,900
Criminal Lawyer	110.107-014	Excellent	39,800
District Attorney	110.117-010	Fair/Good	40,200
Insurance Lawyer	110.117-014	Good/Exc.	33,100
Judge	111.107-010	Fair/Good	65,400
Lawyer	110.107-010	Excellent	35,300
Patent Lawyer	110.117-026	Good	38,900
Probate Lawyer	110.117-030	Excellent	35,000
Professor	090.227-010	Good	38,900
Real Estate Lawyer	110.117-034	Good	33,100
Tax Attorney	110.117-038	Excellent	34,100
Title Attorney	110.117-042	Good	30,600

Occupational Personality Styles: Influencing, Social

DPT Functions: Data = H   People = H   Things = L

GOE Work Groups: Business Administration, Law, Social Research

Library Science

Library work is divided into two areas: user services and technical services. Librarians in user services work directly with the public to help them find the information they need. Technical services librarians are primarily concerned with acquiring and preparing materials for use and deal less frequently with the public. Employment opportunities are available in schools, public libraries, private industry, government agencies, hospitals, correctional facilities, or as consultants or faculty in schools of library science.

COURSE REQUIREMENTS

Acquisition of Materials
Administration
Archives and Manuscripts
Cataloging and Classification
Government Publications
Information Retrieval

Information Systems
Manuscription
Media Center
Organization of Materials
Reference Theory
Research Services

OPTIONS WITHIN MAJOR

Research

Technical Services

RECOMMENDED HIGH SCHOOL COURSES

Art
English
History

Literature
Science

CAREERS	D.O.T. NUMBER	OUTLOOK	AVERAGE INITIAL SALARY
Associate Degree			
Library Technician	100.367-018	Good	$13,300
Bachelor Degrees			
Archivist	101.167-010	Fair	25,100
Audiovisual Librarian	100.167-010	Fair	19,000
Cataloger	100.387-010	Fair	15,100
Classifier	100.367-014	Fair	17,300
Librarian	100.127-014	Good	24,400
Media Specialist	100.167-030	Fair	19,500
Public Librarian	100.127-014	Good	18,300
Reference Librarian	100.267-014	Good	18,300
School Librarian	100.167-030	Good/Exc.	19,500
Graduate Degrees			
Acquisition Librarian	100.267-010	Fair	28,000
Professor	090.227-010	Good	32,900
Special Collections Librarian	100.267-014	Fair	28,100

Occupational Personality Styles: Serving, Detail-oriented

DPT Functions: Data = H   People = L   Things = L

GOE Work Group: Educational and Library Services

Linguistics

With the world sharing more in terms of industry, education, medicine, and science and technology, communications among the countries of the world becomes increasingly important. Technological advancements such as computer translation allow students to study in the more traditional track or specialize in training with computer applications to language. Different from the study of foreign language, linguistics studies the structure and application of language in general.

COURSE REQUIREMENTS

Comparative Linguistics
German
History of English Language
History of Language
Humanities Computing
Junction Grammar
Language Acquisition
Language and Computers
Language and Culture
Latin
Modern Linguistics

Philosophy
Phonology
Psychology and Language
Semantics
Set Theory Mathematics
Spanish
Speech Processing
Syntactic Theory
Translation
Uncommon Languages

OPTIONS WITHIN MAJOR

Business
Computer Translation

International Consulting
Research

RECOMMENDED HIGH SCHOOL COURSES

Computer Science
English (3 years)
Foreign Language

History
Math (3 years)

CAREERS	D.O.T. NUMBER	OUTLOOK	AVERAGE INITIAL SALARY
Bachelor Degrees			
English as a Second Language Instructor	091.227-010	Good	$19,500
Intelligence Expert	059.267-010	Good	25,900
Translator	137.267-018	Good	23,200
Graduate Degrees			
Computer Translator	030.162-010	Excellent	39,500
Professor	090.227-010	Good	32,900
Researcher	199.267-034	Excellent	32,900
Scientific Linguist	059.067-014	Fair	30,000

Occupational Personality Style: Scientific

DPT Functions: Data = H   People = M   Things = L

GOE Work Groups: Communications, Social Research

Manufacturing Engineering Technology

As a chief industry in the United States, manufacturing employs over 19 million people, accounting for over 25 percent of all dollars earned. Manufacturing technology combines engineering and management principles and skills for planning, developing, implementing, and controlling industrial manufacturing processes. The manufacturing technologist analyzes and plans process equipment and facilities required for the fabrication and assembly of products. Increased sophistication of manufacturing with computer-aided techniques has greatly increased the international job market for qualified graduates.

COURSE REQUIREMENTS

Advanced Mechanical Drafting
Applied Mechanics
Applied Physics
Basic Fluid Power
Computer-Aided Graphics
Computer-Aided Manufacturing
Computer Programming
Cost Metal Processes
Economy, Society,
    and Public Policy
Electrical Machines and
    Controls
Industrial Electronics
Industrial Robotics
Machine Tool Performance
Manufacturing
Manufacturing Development

Manufacturing Practicum
Manufacturing Process Planning
Manufacturing Processes
Mechanical Drafting
Metal Forming
Numerical Control Programming
Physical Metallurgy
Plastic Tooling Processing
Production Operations
Production Planning
Quality Assurance
Scientific Computing
Technical Mathematics
Technical Writing
Tool Design
Welding Processes

OPTIONS WITHIN MAJOR

Automated Systems
Computer-Integrated
    Manufacturing

Management
Manufacturing
Welding

RECOMMENDED HIGH SCHOOL COURSES

Algebra	Physics
Algebra II	Trigonometry
Drafting	Woodworking
Machine Shop	

CAREERS	D.O.T. NUMBER	OUTLOOK	AVERAGE INITIAL SALARY
Associate Degrees			
Industrial Laboratory Technician		Excellent	$21,200
Materials Science Technician	029.081-014	Good	17,000
Bachelor Degrees			
Die Designer	007.161-010	Good	23,500
Industrial Engineer	012.167-030	Excellent	29,700
Manufacturing Engineer	012.167-042	Excellent	30,500
Project Engineer	019.167-014	Excellent	25,800
Quality Control Engineer	012.167-054	Excellent	28,500
Tool Designer	007.061-026	Good	28,000
Tool Programmer	007.167-018	Good	27,300
Graduate Degrees			
Computer-Aided Mfg. Consultant		Excellent	35,000
Professor	090.227-010	Excellent	32,900

Occupational Personality Styles:	Scientific, Technical
DPT Functions:	Data = H People = L Things = H
GOE Work Groups:	Engineering Technology, Managerial Work: Mechanical

Marketing and Retailing

Marketing and retailing are necessary in an economy based on business transactions. As the world is more easily traversed regarding international business, this major increases in both impact and complexity. Graduates from this major contribute in retail management, industrial marketing, sales management, forecasting and market research, personnel, merchandising, financial control, and store operations.

COURSE REQUIREMENTS

Accounting
Business Policy
Buying Behavior
Financial Management
Information Management
International Marketing
Management Economics
Market Analysis and Forecasting

Marketing Management
Marketing Models
Marketing Research
Operations Management
Organizational Behavior
Promotion Management
Retail Management
Sales and Distribution

OPTIONS WITHIN MAJOR

Marketing
International Business

Retailing

RECOMMENDED HIGH SCHOOL COURSES

Algebra
English

Geometry
History

CAREERS	D.O.T. NUMBER	OUTLOOK	AVERAGE INITIAL SALARY
Bachelor Degrees			
Buyer	162.157-018	Good	$24,500
Job Analyst	166.267-018	Good	20,000
Market Research Analyst	050.067-014	Excellent	25,100
Personnel Manager	166.167-018	Excellent	30,700
Purchasing Agent	162.157-038	Good/Fair	25,100
Retail Manager	185.167-078	Good/Exc.	23,000
Sales Manager	165.167-018	Good	23,900
Graduate Degrees			
Marketing Retail Analyst	050.067-014	Excellent	40,100
Professor	090.227-010	Good	32,900

Occupational Personality Styles:	Detail-oriented, Scientific, Influencing
DPT Functions:	Data = H People = M Things = L
GOE Work Groups:	Business Management, Mathematics and Statistics

Mathematics

Mathematics is a precise academic discipline which defies simplistic defini-
tion. It is a fundamental tool in education, government, and almost every
other profession or area of study. Elements of language, art, and science are
aspects of math that prepare students for work in business and industry, as
well as in specialized areas of mathematics. Approximately 58 percent of all
professional mathematicians work in management or administration. Many
graduates also pursue other professional or advanced degree studies.

COURSE REQUIREMENTS

Abstract Algebra
Calculus and Analysis
Calculus of Several Variables
Complex Analysis
Differential Equations
Finite Mathematics
Graph Theory
History of Mathematics

Linear Algebra
Matrix Analysis
Numerical Analysis
Numerical Methods Technology
Real Analysis
Set Theory
Theory of Numbers

OPTIONS WITHIN MAJOR

Computational Mathematics
Mathematics

Mathematics Philosophy
Mathematics Science

RECOMMENDED HIGH SCHOOL COURSES

Algebra (2 years)
Calculus
Chemistry
Foreign Language

Geometry
Physics
Trigonometry

CAREERS	D.O.T. NUMBER	OUTLOOK	AVERAGE INITIAL SALARY
Bachelor Degrees			
Actuary	020.167-010	Good/Exc.	$27,500
Auditor	160.167-054	Good/Exc.	26,100
Efficiency Engineer	012.167-070	Fair	24,800
Mathematician	020.067-014	Good	31,400
Navigator	196.167-014	Fair	27,000
Operations Research Analyst	020.067-018	Good	27,000
Psychometrician	045.067-018	Good	27,500
Teacher	091.227-010	Good	19,500
Graduate Degrees			
Auditor	160.167-054	Excellent	32,000
Computer Applications Engineer	020.062-010	Excellent	37,900
Professor	090.227-010	Good	37,900
Statistician	020.067-022	Excellent	30,400
Theoretical Mathematician	020.067-014	Excellent	38,000

Occupational Personality Style:	Scientific
DPT Functions:	Data = H People = L Things = L
GOE Work Groups:	Mathematics and Statistics, Social Research

Mechanical Engineering

Mechanical engineering is the applied science that deals with analysis, design, development, fabrication, and application of products that are predominantly mechanical and energy-related. The field includes many varieties of specialization, from farm machinery to consumer goods (such as automobiles, equipment, and so on). Projected needs in the area of mechanical engineering exceed the number of graduates expected, and job opportunities should remain plentiful in the near future.

COURSE REQUIREMENTS

Aerospace
Analytical Geometry and
  Calculus
Applied Metallurgy
Applied Ordinary Differential
  Equations
Automatic Controls
Bioengineering
College Chemistry
Design for Manufacture Areas
Electrical Engineering
Engineering Graphics
Engineering Mechanics
Fluid Mechanics
Heat Transfer

Kinematics
Manufacture of Machine
  Components
Mechanical Design
Mechanical Engineering
  Instrumentation
Metallurgy
Nuclear Engineering
Numerical Methods
Physics
Solid Mechanic
System Design
Thermodynamics
Vibrations and Dynamics

OPTIONS WITHIN MAJOR

Aerospace
Automatic Controls Systems
  Analysis
Bioengineering

Fluid Mechanics
Heat Transfer
Materials and Metallurgy
Thermodynamics

RECOMMENDED HIGH SCHOOL COURSES

Chemistry　　　　　　　Mechanical Drawing
English (4 years)　　　　Physics
Math (3 years)

CAREERS	D.O.T. NUMBER	OUTLOOK	AVERAGE INITIAL SALARY
Bachelor Degrees			
Automotive Engineer	007.061-010	Good	$27,500
Construction Supervisor		Good/Exc.	28,000
Design Engineer	007.061-018	Good	28,100
Industrial Designer	142.061-026	Good	24,900
Mechanical Engineer	007.061-014	Excellent	29,900
Plant Manager	183.117-010	Good	27,800
Graduate Degrees			
Engineer	007.061-014	Excellent	39,400
Engineering Researcher	024.167-010	Excellent	39,000
Professor	090.227-010	Excellent	32,900

Occupational Personality Styles:　Scientific, Technical

DPT Functions:　　　　　　Data = H　People = L　Things = H

GOE Work Groups:　　　　Engineering, Quality Control, Systems Operation

Medical Technology

Medical technology graduates are prepared in laboratory procedures to assist in the examination and treatment of patients. Some medical technologists do research in laboratory technique or drug exploration, but more than 80 percent perform tests in microbiology, parasitology, biochemistry, blood banking, hematology, histology, or nuclear medical technology in a hospital setting, where opportunities are excellent.

COURSE REQUIREMENTS

Biochemistry
Biology
Botany
Chemistry
College Algebra
Epidemiology
Human Parasitology
Immunology

Medical Technology
Microbiology
Organic Chemistry
Pathogenic Microbiology
Pathophysiology
Physics
Zoology

OPTIONS WITHIN MAJOR

Institutional Care

Laboratory Science

RECOMMENDED HIGH SCHOOL COURSES

Biology
Chemistry
English (4 years)

Math (3 years)
Physics

CAREERS	D.O.T. NUMBER	OUTLOOK	AVERAGE INITIAL SALARY
Associate Degrees			
Dental Technologist	078.361-010	Excellent	$18,500
Dialysis Technician	078.362-014	Excellent	19,500
Electrocardiographic Technician	078.362-018	Good/Exc.	18,700
Electroencephalographic Technician	078.362-022	Good/Exc.	16,100
Medical Laboratory Technician	078.381-014	Excellent	18,900
Radiological Technologist	078.362-026	Excellent	21,500
Respiratory Therapist	076.361-014	Excellent	22,800
Tissue Technologist	078.261-030	Excellent	21,200
Ultrasound Technologist	078.364-010	Excellent	21,300
X-ray Technologist	078.362-026	Excellent	18,300
Bachelor Degrees			
Hospital or Health Service Coordinator		Excellent	26,900
Medical Technologist	078.261-038	Excellent	24,800
Nuclear Medical Technologist	078.361-018	Good	23,900
Orthotist	078.261-018	Good	21,800
Pharmaceutical Salesperson	262.357-010	Good	28,000
Prosthetist	078.261-022	Good	21,900
Graduate Degrees			
Cytotechnologist	078.261-026	Fair	28,000
Hospital Laboratory Education Administrator	187.117-010	Excellent	25,700
Medical Researcher		Excellent	38,000
Professor	090.227-010	Excellent	32,900

Occupational Personality Styles: Scientific, Technical

DPT Functions: Data = H   People = L   Things = M

GOE Work Groups: Laboratory Technology, Life Sciences, Medical Sciences

Medicine

Despite a growing need for medical services, the limited capacities of present medical schools make competition for entrance into the medical field very keen. Only students who score very well on the medical schools' admission test and maintain outstanding grade-point averages are considered for admission. Although the exact sciences are satisfactory in preparing the undergraduate, more and more students are selecting preprofessional majors that can serve as alternates to medical school if they are not selected. Students should pursue a broad general education in addition to the extensive science prerequisites to enhance their possibilities for acceptance into medical schools.

COURSE REQUIREMENTS

Most students accepted to medical school have bachelor's degrees. Courses include the following:

Anatomy   Physiology
Biochemistry   Psychology
Chemistry   Qualitative Analysis
Genetics   Quantitative Analysis
Microbiology   Vertebrate Anatomy
Physics

Professional school courses are a continuation of those above but in more depth and with clinical experience.

RECOMMENDED HIGH SCHOOL COURSES

Biology   Math (3 years)
Chemistry   Physics
English (4 years)   Physiology

CAREERS	D.O.T. NUMBER	OUTLOOK	AVERAGE INITIAL SALARY
Graduate Degrees			
Acupuncturist	079.271-010	Excellent	$ 68,000
Allergist	070.101-102	Excellent	104,000
Anesthesiologist	070.101-010	Excellent	121,000
Cardiologist	070.101-014	Excellent	118,100
Dermatologist	070.101-018	Excellent	100,100
Family Practitioner	070.101-026	Excellent	95,300
General Practitioner	070.101-022	Excellent	95,300
Gynecologist	070.101-034	Excellent	120,000
Internist	070.101-042	Excellent	112,000
Neurologist	070.101-050	Excellent	120,000
Obstetrician	070.101-054	Excellent	120,000
Opthalmologist	070.101-058	Excellent	105,000
Orthopedic Surgeon	070.101-094	Excellent	110,000
Pathologist	070.061-010	Excellent	115,000
Pediatrician	070.101-066	Excellent	101,000
Proctologist	070.101-086	Excellent	105,000
Psychiatrist	070.107-014	Excellent	111,000
Radiologist	070.101-090	Excellent	125,500
Surgeon	070.101-094	Excellent	121,000
Urologist	070.101-098	Excellent	112,000

Occupational Personality Styles: Scientific, Social, Serving

DPT Functions: Data = H   People = H   Things = H

GOE Work Groups: Life Sciences, Medical Sciences

Metallurgical Engineering

Metallurgical engineers develop new types of metal with characteristics that are tailored to meet specific requirements, such as heat resistance, high strength but lightweight, or high malleability. They also develop methods to process and convert metals into useful products.

The metalworking industries—primarily the iron and steel and nonferrous metals industries—employ over one-half the metallurgical and materials engineers. Metallurgical engineers also work in industries that manufacture machinery, electrical equipment, and aircraft parts, and in the mining industries. Some work for government agencies, colleges, and universities.

COURSE REQUIREMENTS

Algebra
Calculus and Analytic Geometry
Chemistry
Computer Programming
Engineering Communications
Engineering Mechanics

Materials Science
Physics
Statistical Methods
Systems Methodology
Thermal-Fluid Phenomena
Trigonometry

OPTIONS WITH MAJOR

Chemical Metallurgy

Physical Metallurgy

RECOMMENDED HIGH SCHOOL COURSES

Chemistry
Drafting
English

Math (3 years)
Physics

CAREERS	D.O.T. NUMBER	OUTLOOK	AVERAGE INITIAL SALARY
Associate Degrees			
Metals/Materials Technician	011.261-010	Excellent	$18,000
Metallurgical Engineering Technician	011.261-010	Excellent	19,500
Bachelor Degrees			
Chemical Metallurgist	011.061-018	Excellent	28,400
Extractive Metallurgist	011.061-018	Good	21,900
Metallographer	110.061-014	Excellent	24,500
Physical Metallurgist	011.061-022	Excellent	30,900
Graduate Degree			
Professor	090.227-010	Excellent	32,900

Occupational Personality Styles: Scientific, Technical

DPT Functions: Data = H   People = L   Things = H

GOE Work Groups: Engineering, Physical Sciences

Microbiology

Microbiology is the study of microscopic forms of life (bacteria, viruses, molds, yeasts, algae, protozoa) used in food and industrial microbiology; immunology; medical microbiology, microbial ecology, and genetics microbial physiology; and virology. Preprofessional students (medical and dental) find microbiology excellent training for their graduate work. Employment opportunities are available in industry, hospitals, government agencies, and universities.

COURSE REQUIREMENTS

Algebra
Bacterial Physiology
Biochemistry
Biology
Chemical Pathology
Chemistry
Epidemiology
Food and Dairy Microbiology
Genetics
Immunology

Microbial Genetics
Microbiology
Organic Chemistry
Pathogenic Microbiology
Pathophysiology
Physics
Statistics
Trigonometry
Virology
Water and Sewage Microbiology

OPTIONS WITHIN MAJOR

Environmental Health Science   Laboratory Services

RECOMMENDED HIGH SCHOOL COURSES

Biology
Chemistry
English

Math (3 years)
Physics

CAREERS	D.O.T. NUMBER	OUTLOOK	AVERAGE INITIAL SALARY
Bachelor Degrees			
Cytotechnologist	078.281-010	Excellent	$20,000
Environmental Health Scientist	029.081-010	Good	18,000
Microbiologist	041.061-058	Good	24,000
Microbiology Technologist	078.261-014	Excellent	21,000
Public Health Scientist	041.261-010	Good	20,500
Quality Control Lab Technician	012.261-014	Fair	18,500
Graduate Degrees			
Cytologist	041.061-042	Fair	28,000
Parasitologist	041.061-070	Good	29,000
Professor	090.227-010	Good	32,900
Researcher	199.267-034	Excellent	33,900

Occupational Personality Style: Scientific

DPT Functions: Data = H   People = L   Things = H

GOE Work Groups: Life Sciences, Laboratory Technology, Medical Sciences

Mining and Geological Engineering

The mining (mineral) engineer works with mineral deposits of all kinds from the time of their discovery through their evaluation and production. Although his chief job is usually to get the most ore out of the ground for the least cost, the mining engineer often works in many other areas, such as research, safety, design, environment, pollution control, and management.

Major metal, mining, and coal companies are leading prospects for jobs for mineral engineers who have strong career convictions and an eye toward possible advancement to management positions. Power and steel companies often own subsidiary companies that also employ mineral engineers. Manufacturers dealing with fertilizers, mining machinery, and equipment are good job opportunities, as are cement companies and quarries of various types.

COURSE REQUIREMENTS

Bulk Materials Handling
Calculus
Drilling and Blasting
Electrical Circuits
Engineering Physics
Environmental Engineering
Fluid Mechanics
Materials Testing
Mechanics of Materials

Metallurgy for Engineers
Mineral Exploitation
Mineralogy
Mining Computations
Petrology
Rock Mechanics
Structural Geology
Surveying

OPTIONS WITHIN MAJOR

Fluid Mechanics
Geology

Mining Engineering

RECOMMENDED HIGH SCHOOL COURSES

Algebra
Chemistry
Geography
Geometry

Mechanical Drawing
Physics
Trigonometry

CAREERS	D.O.T. NUMBER	OUTLOOK	AVERAGE INITIAL SALARY
Associate Degree			
Mining Engineer Technician		Good	$17,200
Bachelor Degrees			
Chief Petroleum Engineer	010.161.014	Excellent	35,000
Mining Engineer	024.161-010	Excellent	28,300
Mining Geologist	024.061-022	Excellent	29,900
Mining Geologist Engineer	024.061-019	Excellent	32,900
Graduate Degrees			
Professor	090.227-010	Excellent	32,900
Researcher	199.267-034	Excellent	35,200

Occupational Personality Styles: Scientific, Technical

DPT Functions: Data = H   People = L   Things = H

GOE Work Groups: Engineering, Quality Control, Systems Operation

Music

Music includes the study of theory, composition, arrangement, teaching, and performance. Graduates may pursue careers as skilled performers in the concert or professional world, as music teachers in elementary or secondary schools, or on a private basis. Teaching opportunities are still good in many areas but arranging, composing, directing, and conducting openings are very limited.

COURSE REQUIREMENTS

Analytical Techniques
Essentials of Conducting
History of Music
Music Theory
Pedagogy

Performance Instruction
Private Instruction
Recital
Survey Music Literature

OPTIONS WITHIN MAJOR

Composition
Education
Music Theory

Performance
Piano Technician

RECOMMENDED HIGH SCHOOL COURSES

Band
Choral
Music Composition

Music Theory
Private Lessons

The Career Connection for College Education

CAREERS	D.O.T. NUMBER	OUTLOOK	AVERAGE INITIAL SALARY
Associate Degree			
Piano Technician	730.281-038	Good	$12,000
Bachelor Degrees			
Arranger	152.067-010	Poor	21,100
Composer	152.067-014	Poor	29,600
Music Copyist	209.582-010	Fair/Good	22,300
Music Director, Instructor	152.021-010	Fair/Good	27,000
Music Director, TV	100.367-022	Fair/Good	25,200
Music Therapist	076.127-014	Fair	18,000
Performer	152.041-010	Fair/Good	Varies
Teacher	152.021-010	Good	19,500
Graduate Degrees			
Conductor	152.047-014	Poor	32,100
Professor	090.227-010	Excellent	32,900

Occupational Personality Styles: Artistic, Influencing, Social

DPT Functions: Data = H   People = M   Things = H

GOE Work Groups: Educational and Library Services, Performing Arts: Music

Near Eastern Studies

Near Eastern studies is an interdisciplinary program typically referred to as "area studies." It integrates ideas and principles from anthropology, literature, history, geography, and economics. This broadly based education allows one to do historical research; social, political, and economic analysis; and literary criticism. Students often continue on to advanced studies in law, business administration, or liberal arts, or may become involved in teaching or government service.

COURSE REQUIREMENTS

Ancient Egypt and Mesopotamia
Arab-Israeli Conflict
Asiatic Russia
Biblical Archaeology
Geography of the Near East
Humanities of the Islamic World
Humanities of the Near East

Islamic Philosophy and Religion
Jewish Philosophy and Religion
Near Eastern Archaeology
Near Eastern History
Peoples of the Middle East
Political Systems
Studies in Ancient Languages

OPTIONS WITHIN MAJOR

International Politics

Religion/Philosophy

RECOMMENDED HIGH SCHOOL COURSES

Art
Economics
English
Foreign Language

Geography
History
Literature

CAREERS	D.O.T. NUMBER	OUTLOOK	AVERAGE INITIAL SALARY
Bachelor Degrees			
Biographer	052.067-010	Fair/Poor	Varies
Correspondent	131.267-018	Fair	$24,000
Foreign-Service Officer	188.117-106	Fair	25,100
Historian	052.067-022	Fair/Poor	25,200
Import/Export Agent	184.117-022	Good	23,100
Intelligence Expert	059.267-010	Good	25,900
Public Relations Specialist	165.167-014	Fair	29,100
Publications Editor	132.037-022	Poor	25,300
Travel Agent	252.152-010	Good	17,200
Graduate Degrees			
Foreign Service	051.067-010	Good	30,100
Professor	090.227-010	Good	32,900
Researcher	199.267-034	Good	30,000

Occupational Personality Styles: Social, Scientific

DPT Functions: Data = H   People = M   Things = L

GOE Work Group: Social Research

Nursing

Nurses are constantly in demand as an integral part of the health service professions. Hospitals, clinics, public health agencies, armed services, schools, and comprehensive mental health centers find the skills and assistance of qualified nurses indispensable. Besides a need for undergraduate nurses, there is a great demand for nurses with advanced education as clinicians, specialists, researchers, teachers, and administrators. Excellent employment service opportunities exist for men and women throughout the nation and in foreign countries as well.

COURSE REQUIREMENTS

Biophysical Assessment
Chemistry
Child Development
Clinical Care
College Algebra
Community Health
Emergency
Essentials in Nutrition
Family Health Management
Human Anatomy
Intensive Care
Medical-Surgical Practices
Microbiology
Obstetrics
Pathology
Patient Relationships
Pharmacology
Preceptorship
Primary Care
Psychiatric Nursing
Psychology
Psychosocial Nursing
Research
Social Psychology

OPTIONS WITHIN MAJOR

Clinical Nursing
Institutional Nursing
Nursing Administration

RECOMMENDED HIGH SCHOOL COURSES

Algebra
Biology
Chemistry
English
Geometry
Physics
Physiology
Psychology

CAREERS	D.O.T. NUMBER	OUTLOOK	AVERAGE INITIAL SALARY
Associate Degree			
Licensed Practical Nurse	079.374-014	Excellent	$16,200
Bachelor Degrees			
Industrial Nurse	075.117-020	Excellent	27,500
Nurse Anesthetist	075.371-010	Excellent	55,000
Nurse Instructor	075.124-018	Excellent	27,900
Nurse Midwife	075.264-014	Good	23,000
Public Health Nurse	075.124-014	Good	20,100
Public Health Nutritionist	077.127-010	Good/Exc.	23,000
Registered Nurse	075.364-010	Excellent	26,300
Graduate Degrees			
Nurse Supervisor	075.167-010	Excellent	35,000
Professor	090.227-010	Excellent	32,900

Occupational Personality Styles: Serving, Scientific, Technical

DPT Functions: Data = H   People = H   Things = H

GOE Work Groups: Life Sciences, Medical Sciences, Nursing, Therapy, and Specialized Teaching Services

Occupational Health and Safety

The occupational health and safety field recognizes, evaluates, and controls health and safety hazards in industry. Specific hazard areas of radiation, toxic gases, fumes, dusts, noise ergonomics, and safety are the concern of the occupational hygienist. Employment opportunities are excellent within various industries and public health agencies.

COURSE REQUIREMENTS

Computer Science
Epidemiology
Human Physiology
Leadership Development
Occupational Health
  Instrumentation

Occupational/Industrial Health
Organic Chemistry
Organizational Behavior
Physics
Safety Education

OPTIONS WITHIN MAJOR

Industrial Health and Safety

Occupational Health and Safety

RECOMMENDED HIGH SCHOOL COURSES

Biology
Chemistry
English

Math
Physiology

CAREERS	D.O.T. NUMBER	OUTLOOK	AVERAGE INITIAL SALARY
Bachelor Degrees			
Environmental Health Specialist	029.261-014	Good	$18,000
Industrial Hygienist	079.161-010	Fair	31,200
Industrial Health Engr.	012.167-034	Good	28,700
Occupational Safety Inspector	168.167-062	Fair/Good	22,100
Safety Manager	012.167-058	Fair	24,000

Occupational Personality Styles: Technical, Serving, Scientific

DPT Functions: Data = H   People = M   Things = L

GOE Work Groups: Hospitality Services, Medical Sciences, Safety and Law Enforcement

Occupational Therapy

Occupational therapists assist people in special situations in preparing themselves for job entry. Handicapped students are assisted by career assessments followed by placement programs. Other settings for this career are mental health agencies and hospitals.

COURSE REQUIREMENTS

Career Assessment
Career Counseling
Correctional Physical Education
Counseling
Group Dynamics
Heredity
Human Growth and
  Development

Job Placement
Psychometrics
Psychosocial Dysfunctions
Special Education
Statistics
Technical Writing
Work Evaluation

Often a bachelor's degree is needed to apply for the competitive acceptance into professional (graduate) school.

OPTION WITHIN MAJOR

Physical Therapy

RECOMMENDED HIGH SCHOOL COURSES

English
Math (2 years)

Sociology

CAREERS	D.O.T. NUMBER	OUTLOOK	AVERAGE INITIAL SALARY
Bachelor Degrees			
Counselor	045.107-010	Good/Exc.	$23,900
Occupational Therapist	076.121-010	Excellent	25,800

Occupational Personality Styles: Serving, Technical

DPT Functions: Data = H   People = H   Things = H

GOE Work Groups: Social Research, Social Services

Oceanography

Oceanographers use the principles and techniques of natural science, mathematics, and engineering to study oceans—their movements, physical properties, and plant and animal life. Their research not only extends basic scientific knowledge, but also helps develop practical methods for forecasting weather, developing fisheries, mining ocean resources, and improving national defense. Oceanographers find job opportunities available in colleges and universities, and in the federal government. Federal agencies employing substantial numbers of oceanographers include the navy and the National Oceanic and Atmospheric Administration. Some oceanographers work in private industry, and a few work for fishery laboratories of state and local governments.

COURSE REQUIREMENTS

Biological Oceanography
Chemical Oceanography
Chemistry
Geology
Geophysics
Life Support and Diving
  Technology

Meteorology
Ocean Engineering
Ocean Measurements
Oceanography
Physical Oceanography
Physics

OPTIONS WITHIN MAJOR

Biological Oceanography
Chemical Oceanography

Geological Oceanography
Physical Oceanography

RECOMMENDED HIGH SCHOOL COURSES

Biology
Chemistry
English

Math (3 years)
Physics
Physiology

CAREERS	D.O.T. NUMBER	OUTLOOK	AVERAGE INITIAL SALARY
Bachelor Degree			
Marine Biologist	041.061-022	Good	$25,100
Graduate Degrees			
Geographer	029.067-010	Good	28,000
Marine Geologist	024.061-018	Excellent	28,300
Oceanographic Engineer		Fair/Poor	28,000
Physical Geographer	029.067-014	Good	28,100
Physical Oceanographer	024.061-030	Good	26,500
Professor	090.227-010	Good	32,900

Occupational Personality Styles: Scientific, Technical

DPT Functions: Data = H   People = L   Things = M

GOE Work Groups: Mathematics and Statistics, Physical Sciences

Optometry

An optometrist assists people with visual defects to see efficiently by making tests and prescribing visual aids (which do not require drugs or surgery). Eighty percent of the optometrists in the United States are self-employed. Employment opportunities continue to grow as the population's eye-care needs increase. A student's grade-point average is of prime importance in consideration for graduate school.

COURSE REQUIREMENTS

There are 13 optometry schools in the United States and Canada requiring course work in the following in order to be accepted:

Anatomy	Physics
Biochemistry	Physiology
Chemistry	Psychology
English	Vertebrate Anatomy
Math	Zoology
Microbiology	

RECOMMENDED HIGH SCHOOL COURSES

Algebra	Geometry
Chemistry	Physics
English	Physiology

CAREER	D.O.T. NUMBER	OUTLOOK	AVERAGE INITIAL SALARY
Graduate Degree			
Optometrist	079.101-018	Excellent	$33,800

Occupational Personality Styles:	Serving, Technical, Scientific
DPT Functions:	Data = H People = M Things = H
GOE Work Groups:	Laboratory Technology, Life Sciences, Medical Sciences

Pharmacy

Pharmacy is a health profession dealing with the preparation and distribution of drugs and medicines prescribed by practitioners. Besides knowing the chemistry of compounds and their effects on human beings, a pharmacist is generally required to understand sound business management and personnel supervision. Large pharmaceutical firms and drugstores make up the majority of job opportunities in this field.

COURSE REQUIREMENTS

Three to four years of undergraduate programs are needed to enter professional school. Undergraduate courses include:

Algebra
Anatomy
Biochemistry
Chemistry
English

Math
Microbiology
Physics
Physiology

Professional schools require different courses for entrance. They continue the same types of courses but are more specialized and detailed.

RECOMMENDED HIGH SCHOOL COURSES

Algebra
Biology
Chemistry

English
Geometry
Physiology

CAREER	D.O.T. NUMBER	OUTLOOK	AVERAGE INITIAL SALARY
Graduate Degree			
Pharmacist	074.161-010	Good	$43,900

Occupational Personality Styles:	Technical, Detail-oriented, Scientific
DPT Functions:	Data = H People = L Things = H
GOE Work Groups:	Laboratory Sciences, Life Sciences, Medical Sciences

Philosophy

Philosophy fosters creative and critical thinking and helps one to understand human thought through the ages. Students often major in another discipline at the same time they are studying philosophy. This joint-major program is excellent preparation for law and other preprofessional programs.

COURSE REQUIREMENTS

Aesthetics
Ancient and Medieval Origins
   of Western Philosophy
Directed Readings in Philosophy
The Emergence of Modern
   Philosophy
Epistemology
Ethics
Evaluation Arguments and
   Evidence
Figures in Philosophy
Foundations of Philosophical
   Thought
Graduate Seminar
Intermediate Logic
Logic and Language
Metaphysics
Philosophy of Religion
Readings in Philosophy
Topics in Philosophy

RECOMMENDED HIGH SCHOOL COURSES

English
Forensics
Languages
Math
Philosophy

CAREERS	D.O.T. NUMBER	OUTLOOK	AVERAGE INITIAL SALARY
Bachelor Degrees			
Clergy	120.107-010	Good	$26,000
Editorial Writer	131.067-022	Fair	25,200
Graduate Degrees			
Critic	131.067-018	Fair	34,700
Professor	090.227-010	Fair	32,900

Occupational Personality Styles: Scientific, Influencing

DPT Functions: Data = H   People = L   Things = L

GOE Work Groups: Communications, Social Research

Physical Education

An increasing emphasis on physical fitness throughout the country has opened new opportunities for physical education graduates as athletic directors in sports clubs, exercise specialists in health clubs, and athletic trainers in amateur and professional teams. Still, the major source of employment is teaching and coaching in public and private schools and universities, with many and varied opportunities in sports and dance. Several students continue on in graduate work to do research or become administrators of various athletic interests.

COURSE REQUIREMENTS

Adaptive and Corrective Physical Education
Advanced Life Saving
Child Development
Diagnosis of Athletic Injuries
Human Anatomy
Human Physiology
Motor Learning
Physical Education
Physical Education for Teachers
Sports Fundamentals
Statistics

OPTIONS WITHIN MAJOR

Athletic Training
Coaching
Elementary Education
Intramural Sports
Secondary Education
Special Education

RECOMMENDED HIGH SCHOOL COURSES

Biology
Extramural Sports
Intramural Sports
Math
Physiology

CAREERS	D.O.T. NUMBER	OUTLOOK	AVERAGE INITIAL SALARY
Bachelor Degrees			
Athletic Manager, College	153.117-014	Poor	$25,100
Athletic Trainer	152.224-010	Excellent	18,400
Coach, High School	153.227-010	Fair/Good	23,500
Exercise Specialist		Good/Fair	16,500
Physical Education Teacher	091.227-010	Fair/Good	19,500
Recreation Director	187.167-238	Good	16,800
Graduate Degrees			
Athletic Director	090.117-022	Fair	35,900
Exercise Physiologist	076.121-018	Excellent	38,900
Intramural Sports Director	184.167-034	Fair	25,000
Professor	090.227-010	Fair/Good	32,900
Researcher	199.267-034	Good	30,000
Sports Psychologist		Good	34,600

Occupational Personality Styles: Technical, Serving

DPT Functions: Data = H   People = H   Things = H

GOE Work Groups: Educational and Library Services, Sports

Physical Therapy

Physical therapists work with disabled individuals who suffer handicaps from illness, accident, or birth. The therapist evaluates neuromuscular, musculo-skeletal, sensorimotor, and related cardiovascular and respiratory functions of the patient. Besides evaluation, the therapist supervises activities to increase muscle strength, motor development, functional capacity, and circulatory and respiratory efficiency. The preprofessional program prepares students to enter professional schools in their respective interests. Job opportunities are excellent in hospitals, clinics, or private practice.

COURSE REQUIREMENTS

Body Responses to Health
   and Disease
Chemistry
Health of the Body Systems
Heredity
Human Physiology and
   Anatomy
Microbiology

Physics
Physiology of Activity
Precalculus Mathematics
Rehabilitation Technology
Statistics
Technical Writing
Vertebrate Zoology

Often a bachelor's degree is needed to apply for the competitive acceptance into professional (graduate) school.

OPTION WITHIN MAJOR

Prephysical Therapy

RECOMMENDED HIGH SCHOOL COURSES

Biology
Chemistry
English (3 Years)
History

Math (2 years)
Physiology
Social Problems

CAREERS	D.O.T. NUMBER	OUTLOOK	AVERAGE INITIAL SALARY
Graduate Degrees			
Physical Therapist	076.121-014	Excellent	$29,100
Professor	090.227-010	Good	32,900
Researcher	199.267-034	Good	31,000

Occupational Personality Styles: Technical, Scientific, Serving

DPT Functions: Data = H   People = H   Things = H

GOE Work Groups: Life Sciences, Medical Sciences

Physics and Astronomy

Physics inquires into the nature of the physical world and the laws governing our universe and is, thus, basic to the physical sciences, engineering, technology, and the life sciences. Physicists observe various forms of energy and matter and their relationships in research that investigates the behavior of forces at work within the universe. The career objectives in physics are broad, including scientific research, teaching, engineering, business, law, health, and related fields. Demand for well-trained physicists should increase, especially in applied areas, but many graduates (especially in astronomy) find they must go on to advanced training to prepare for job opportunities.

COURSE REQUIREMENTS

Acoustics
Analytical Geometry and
   Calculus
Astrophysics
Classical Field Theory
Descriptive Astronomy
Differential Equations
Electricity and Magnetism
Environmental Physics
Experimental Physics

Mechanics
Nuclear Theory
Optics and Electromagnetic Theory
Physics
Plasma Physics
Quantum Mechanics
Quantum Theory
Space and Planetary Physics
Theoretical Physics
Thermal Physics

OPTIONS WITHIN MAJOR

Applied Physics
Astronomy

Education
Theoretical Physics

RECOMMENDED HIGH SCHOOL COURSES

Algebra (2 years)
Chemistry
Foreign Language

Geometry
Physics
Trigonometry

CAREERS	D.O.T. NUMBER	OUTLOOK	AVERAGE INITIAL SALARY
Bachelor Degrees			
Electro-optical Engineer	023.061-010	Good	$27,800
Health Physicist	015.021-010	Good	23,600
Meteorologist	025.062-010	Good/Fair	19,500
Solid-State Physicist	023.061-014	Good/Exc.	26,900
Teacher	091.227-010	Good	19,500
Graduate Degrees			
Astronomer	021.067-010	Fair/Good	29,000
Astrophysicist	023.061-014	Good	34,900
Biophysicist	041.061-034	Good	33,400
Chemical Physicist		Good	29,000
Electronic Physicist	023.026-014	Good/Exc.	34,500
Geophysicist	024.061-030	Excellent	31,600
Physicist	023.061-014	Good/Exc.	28,300
Plasma Physicist	023.061-014	Good	30,600
Professor	090.227-010	Fair	32,900
Theoretical Physicist	023.067-010	Excellent	35,900
Writer, Researcher	199.267-034	Good/Exc.	32,900

Occupational Personality Styles: Scientific, Technical

DPT Functions: Data = H   People = L   Things = M

GOE Work Groups: Laboratory Technology, Mathematics and Statistics, Physical Sciences

Political Science

Political scientists study political behavior and institutions. Although some specialize in political theory or philosophy, most political scientists, particularly those specializing in public administration, concern themselves with the organization and operation of government at all levels in the United States and abroad. They explore such phenomena as public opinion, political parties, elections, and special interest groups. They also focus on the workings of the bureaucracy, the presidency, congress, and the judicial system. Processes and techniques of public administration and public policy-making also are concerns of political scientists.

Approximately 80 percent of political scientists work in colleges or universities. Others work for government agencies, consulting firms, political organizations, research institutes, public interest groups, or business firms.

COURSE REQUIREMENTS

Comparative Politics
Comparative Studies
Constitutional Law
Foreign Area Studies
Foreign Policy
Government and Politics
International Law
International Politics

Public Administration and Policy
Political Behavior
Political Theory
Public Policy
State and Local Government
Urban Affairs
U.S. Politics

OPTIONS WITHIN MAJOR

Justice Administration
Political Science

Public Policy

RECOMMENDED HIGH SCHOOL COURSES

American Government
English (4 years)

History
Political Science

CAREERS	D.O.T. NUMBER	OUTLOOK	AVERAGE INITIAL SALARY
Bachelor Degrees			
Columnist	131.067-010	Fair	$21,000
Correspondent	131.267-018	Fair	25,100
Foreign-Service Officer	188.117-106	Fair	22,000
Law Enforcement Trainee		Fair	16,000
Graduate Degrees			
Foreign Service	051.067-010	Good	25,900
Political Scientist	051.067.010	Good	25,000
Professor	090.227-010	Good	32,900
Research	199.267-034	Fair	30,000

Occupational Personality Styles: Influencing, Scientific

DPT Functions: Data = H   People = H   Things = L

GOE Work Groups: Business Administration, Social Research

Portuguese

Like many language studies, Portuguese offers the graduate a variety of vocational opportunities as well as an understanding and appreciation for another language, culture, and people. Many graduate schools and professional studies (law, dentistry, medicine) require a second language, and many students consider language studies good training for further education. International law and business are also open to graduates as well as teaching on the secondary and college level. Owing to the limited number of teaching positions (especially on the high school level), many graduates are prepared for alternatives.

COURSE REQUIREMENTS

Composition
Conversation
Cultural Civilization
Grammar

Literature
Phonetics
Portuguese
Translation

OPTIONS WITHIN MAJOR

Business
Education

Interpretation/Translation

RECOMMENDED HIGH SCHOOL COURSES

Foreign Language
Geography
History

Humanities
Literature
Social Science

CAREERS	D.O.T. NUMBER	OUTLOOK	AVERAGE INITIAL SALARY
Bachelor Degrees			
Customs Official	168.267-022	Fair	$16,500
Foreign-Service Officer	188.117-106	Fair	25,100
Import/Export Agent	184.117-022	Good	23,100
Intelligence Expert	059.267-010	Good	25,900
Interpreter	137.267-014	Fair/Good	23,100
Language Researcher	059.067-014	Fair	25,900
Public Relations Specialist	165.167-014	Fair/Good	29,100
Scientific Writer	131.267-026	Fair	25,300
Teacher	091.227-010	Poor	19,500
Translator	137.267-018	Good	20,000
Travel Agent	252.152-010	Good	17,200
Graduate Degrees			
Professor	090.227-010	Good	32,900
Scientific Linguist	059.067-014	Fair	30,000

Occupational Personality Styles:	Scientific, Social
DPT Functions:	Data = H People = M Things = L
GOE Work Groups:	Business Administration, Business Management, Educational and Library Services, Security Services

Psychology

Psychology is the science that deals with the study of human behavior in a clinical, social, physiological, humanistic, and experimental way. Careers are available in secondary teaching, school counseling, clinical services, and industry. Advanced degrees are usually required for most opportunities, but high school teaching, probation work, psychometry, and various social services are open to those with a bachelor's degree. Graduate students in education, law, medicine, business, public administration, and social work find psychology a valuable undergraduate major.

COURSE REQUIREMENTS

Abnormal Psychology
Adolescent Psychology
Adult Psychology
Child Psychology
Clinical Psychology
Cognitive Processes
Developmental Psychology
Environmental Psychology
Exceptional Children
Leadership
Learning
Mental Disorders

Motivation
Organizational Psychology
Personality
Personnel Psychology
Psychobiology
Psychological Statistics
Psychological Testing
Research and Design
Sensation and Perception
Social Adjustment
Social Psychology

OPTIONS WITHIN MAJOR

Clinical Psychology
Counseling Psychology

Industrial Psychology
Social Psychology

RECOMMENDED HIGH SCHOOL COURSES

Algebra
English
Math

Psychology
Social Science

CAREERS	D.O.T. NUMBER	OUTLOOK	AVERAGE INITIAL SALARY
Bachelor Degrees			
Community Organization Officer	195.167-010	Fair	$17,500
Employment Counselor	045.107-010	Fair	18,600
Manual Arts Therapist	076.124-010	Fair	23,100
Probation/Parole Officer	195.107-046	Good	25,700
Recreational Therapist	076.124-014	Fair	19,500
Teacher	091.227-010	Good	19,500
Graduate Degrees			
Clinical Psychologist	045.107-022	Good/Exc.	31,700
Counseling Psychologist	045.107-026	Good	31,700
Educational Psychologist	045.067-010	Good	27,700
Engineering Psychologist	045.061-014	Fair	31,400
Experimental Psychologist	045.061-018	Good	27,700
Industrial Psychologist	045.107-030	Good	31,400
Industrial Psychometrist	045.067-018	Good	31,000
Industrial Therapist	076.167-010	Fair	28,900
Probation Officer	195.107-046	Good	28,700
Professor	090.227-010	Good	32,900
School Psychologist	045.107-034	Good	26,000
Social Psychologist	045.067-014	Good	26,000
Sports Psychologist		Good	34,600

Occupational Personality Styles: Scientific, Social, Serving

DPT Functions: Data = H   People = H   Things = L

GOE Work Groups: Social Research, Social Services

Public Administration

This professional program is designed to prepare qualified students for rewarding careers in public management and administration. The acquisition of attributes leading to positions of leadership in city, regional, state, and federal agencies is stressed. Many programs require internships, allowing the students to receive structured practical training.

COURSE REQUIREMENTS

Auditing and Evaluation
Budgeting
Business Ethics
Business Government Relations
City Planning and Development
Collective Bargaining
Cost Analysis
Debt Management
Equal Employment Opportunity
Financing Public Services
Investment Funds
Labor Relations
Managerial Economics
Manpower Planning
Oral Communication

Organizational Development
Personnel Management
Public Administration
Public Policy Analysis
Public Works
Quantitative Analysis
Sanitation
Systems Analysis
Tax Policy
Transportation
Urban and Regional Planning
Urban Management
Water Systems
Written Communication

OPTIONS WITHIN MAJOR

Finance
Government Administration
Personnel

Planning
Public Works

RECOMMENDED HIGH SCHOOL COURSES

Algebra
English

History

CAREERS	D.O.T. NUMBER	OUTLOOK	AVERAGE INITIAL SALARY
Bachelor Degrees			
Budget/Management Analyst	160.162-022	Good/Exc.	$25,100
Buyer	162.157-018	Good	24,500
Personnel Manager	166.167-018	Excellent	30,700
Purchasing Agent	162.157-038	Good/Fair	25,100
Safety Manager	012.167-014	Fair	24,000
Graduate Degrees			
Airport Manager	184.117-026	Fair	35,400
Director of Public Services	188.117-030	Fair	31,000
Director of Transportation	184.117-014	Fair	31,000
Professor	090.227-010	Good	32,900
Systems Analyst	030.167-014	Good	39,000

Occupational Personality Styles:	Influencing, Social
DPT Functions:	Data = H People = H Things = L
GOE Work Groups:	Business Administration, Business Management, Services Administration

Public Relations

Public relations workers help businesses, government, universities, and other organizations build and maintain a positive public image. Public relations workers put together information that keeps the public aware of their employer's policies, activities, and accomplishments, and keeps management aware of public attitudes.

Manufacturing firms, public utilities and transportation companies, insurance companies, and trade and professional associations employ many public relations workers.

A sizable number work for government agencies, religious organizations, schools, colleges and universities, museums, health fields, and other human service organizations.

COURSE REQUIREMENTS

Advertising
Broadcasting
Business Administration
Communications
Creative Writing
Illustrative Photography
Journalism
Mass Communications
Media Design
Media Planning

Media Sales
Organizational Communication
Political Science
Psychology
Public Relations Management
Public Relations Theory and
 Techniques
Speech Composition
Writing and Production

OPTIONS WITHIN MAJOR

Business Administration
Education

Private Consulting

RECOMMENDED HIGH SCHOOL COURSES

Business Courses
English (4 years)
Journalism

Political Science
Psychology
Public Speaking

CAREERS	D.O.T. NUMBER	OUTLOOK	AVERAGE INITIAL SALARY
Bachelor Degrees			
Fund-Raiser	293.157-010	Good	$35,000
Lobbyist	165.017-010	Fair	37,000
Promotion Manager	165.167-010	Good	23,500
Public Relations Staff	165.167-014	Good/Exc.	20,000
Graduate Degrees			
Administrator		Good/Exc.	38,000
Consultant	189.167-010	Good	39,000
Managerial	189.167-022	Good/Exc.	31,000
Professor	090.227-010	Excellent	32,900
University Relations		Fair	32,000

Occupational Personality Styles:	Influencing, Social
DPT Functions:	Data = H People = H Things = L
GOE Work Groups:	Business Management, Promotion

Range Management

Range management is sometimes called range science, range ecology, or range conservation. Professionals manage, improve, and protect range resources to maximize their use without damaging the environment. Employment opportunities are available in the federal government, principally in the Forest Service and the Soil Conservation Service of the Department of Agriculture, and the Bureau of Indian Affairs and the Bureau of Land Management in the Department of the Interior. Other opportunities exist in state land agencies, extension services, private industries, consulting firms, and large ranches.

COURSE REQUIREMENTS

Animal Nutrition
Biology
Chemistry
Computer Science
Conservation
Economics
Forestry
Hydrology
Inventory and Analysis
Law Enforcement

Livestock Management
Math
Physics
Plant Ecology
Range Ecology
Range Plants
Resource Management
Soil Science
Watershed Management
Wildlife Management

OPTIONS WITHIN MAJOR

Agribusiness
Range Resources

Wildlife Resources

RECOMMENDED HIGH SCHOOL COURSES

Agriculture
Biology
Chemistry

English (3 years)
Math (2 years)
Speech

CAREERS	D.O.T. NUMBER	OUTLOOK	AVERAGE INITIAL SALARY
Bachelor Degrees			
Agricultural Appraiser	188.167-014	Good	$22,000
Farm Manager	096.127-018	Poor	22,600
Range Manager	040.061-046	Fair	17,900
Vocational Agricultural Teacher	091.221-010	Fair	19,500
Graduate Degrees			
Professor	090.227-010	Good	32,900
Research	199.267-034	Good/Exc.	33,000

Occupational Personality Styles: Technical, Scientific, Influencing

DPT Functions: Data = H   People = M   Things = H

GOE Work Groups: Business Administration, Life Sciences, Managerial Work: Plants and Animals

Recreation Management

A career in recreation is a flexible opportunity of service to people in community centers, commercial organizations, hospitals, and the military. Increased leisure time and rising levels of per capita income for Americans will continue the demand for recreational activities throughout the nation. Graduates who enjoy indoor and outdoor activities, working with a variety of people, and planning and organizing will find adequate employment opportunities in recreational programs.

COURSE REQUIREMENTS

Aging and Leisure
Camp Aquatics
Community Recreation
Community Relations
Crafts for Recreation
Executive Dynamics
Facility Planning
Family Recreation
Land Survival
Leadership

Leisure in Contemporary Society
Mountaineering
Outdoor Recreation
Program Management
Public Facility Management
Skills Training
Social Recreation Leadership
Therapeutic Recreation
Youth Leadership

OPTIONS WITHIN MAJOR

Outdoor Recreation
Scouting

Youth Leadership

RECOMMENDED HIGH SCHOOL COURSES

Business
Crafts
Drama
Music

Psychology
Sociology
Speech

CAREERS	D.O.T. NUMBER	OUTLOOK	AVERAGE INITIAL SALARY
Bachelor Degrees			
Boy Scout Professional	153.117-018	Fair	$21,500
Hotel and Restaurant Administrator	187.117-038	Good	19,100
Hotel Recreation Manager	187.167-122	Fair	18,200
Industrial Recreation Director		Fair	19,000
Municipal Recreation Administrator	187.117-042	Fair	29,300
Outdoor Recreation Director	195.167-026	Fair	16,000
Recreation Supervisor	187.167-238	Good	16,800
Recreational Therapist	076.124-014	Fair	19,500
Graduate Degree			
Professor	090.227-010	Fair/Good	32,900

Occupational Personality Styles:	Social, Influencing
DPT Functions:	Data = H People = H Things = M
GOE Work Groups:	Business Management, Hospitality Services, Services Administration

Russian

Increased interaction with the former Soviet Union in science, industry, and government has escalated the need for trained graduates skilled in the Russian language. Apart from these practical language applications, a tremendous cultural wealth is contained in Russian literature and history. Currently, graduates are finding employment through teaching, government services, business, library work, and language-related research, although many find Russian useful in preparation for graduate school or professional studies.

COURSE REQUIREMENTS

Composition
Conversation
Cultural Civilization
Grammar

Literature
Phonetics
Russian
Translation

OPTIONS WITHIN MAJOR

Business
Education

Interpretation/Translation

RECOMMENDED HIGH SCHOOL COURSES

Foreign Language
Geography
History

Humanities
Literature
Social Science

CAREERS	D.O.T. NUMBER	OUTLOOK	AVERAGE INITIAL SALARY
Bachelor Degrees			
Customs Official	168.267-022	Fair	$16,500
Foreign-Service Officer	188.117-106	Fair	24,000
Import/Export Agent	184.117-022	Good	25,100
Intelligence Expert	059.267-010	Good	25,200
Interpreter	137.267-014	Fair/Good	23,100
Language Researcher	059.067-014	Fair	25,900
Public Relations Specialist	165.167-014	Fair/Good	29,100
Scientific Writer	131.267-026	Good	26,500
Teacher	091.227-010	Poor	19,500
Translator	137.267-018	Good	20,000
Travel Agent	252.152-010	Good	17,200
Graduate Degrees			
Professor	090.227-010	Good	32,900
Scientific Linguist	059.067-014	Fair	30,000

Occupational Personality Styles: Scientific, Social

DPT Functions: Data = H   People = M   Things = L

GOE Work Groups: Business Administration, Business Management, Educational and Library Services, Security Services

Secondary Education

Education in the public schools is a most important concern for over 15 million students and their parents and supplies jobs for over one million teachers. All 50 states require certification in a teaching major and minor. Approved academic majors and minors are those subjects taught in the public schools. Openings are very competitive in the subjects that are not as widely taught or those areas with a surplus of qualified teachers. Vocational and special education are two areas of growing concern and opportunity. Teaching careers in music, foreign languages, art, physical education, and social studies find competition much keener.

COURSE REQUIREMENTS

Contemporary Issues
Educational Law
Educational Philosophy
Foundations in Reading
Individualized Instruction
Research Design
Secondary Curriculum

Secondary Teacher Education
Social Foundations
Specific Courses in Teaching Major
Student Teaching
Teacher Aide Field Study
Teaching Fundamentals
Theory of Teaching

OPTIONS WITHIN MAJOR

Art
Chemistry
Computers
Economics
English
English as a Second Language
French
German
Geography
Geology
Health
History
Home Economics

Industrial Arts
Journalism
Latin
Math
Music
Physical Education
Physics
Political Science
Psychology
Sociology
Spanish
Speech
Theater Arts

RECOMMENDED HIGH SCHOOL COURSES

English (4 years)   Math (2 years)
History   Science

CAREERS	D.O.T. NUMBER	OUTLOOK	AVERAGE INITIAL SALARY
Bachelor Degrees			
Learning Specialist		Fair/Good	$19,500
Remedial Teacher	094.227-030	Good	19,500
Teacher	091.227-010	Good/Exc.	19,500
Graduate Degrees			
Educational Administrator	009.117-026	Fair/Good	53,600
Principal	099.117-018	Fair	53,600
Professor	090.227-010	Fair	32,900

Occupational Personality Styles: Serving, Social

DPT Functions: Data = H   People = H   Things = L

GOE Work Group: Educational and Library Services

Social Work

Social work in the health field involves programs and services that meet the special needs of the ill, disabled, elderly, or otherwise handicapped. Social workers deal with the emotional, social, cultural, and physical needs of patients in whom the effects of illness go far beyond bodily discomfort.

Sixty percent of all social workers provide direct services for public and voluntary agencies, including state departments of public assistance and community welfare and religious organizations. Most of the remainder are involved in social policy and planning, community organization, and administration in governmental agencies, primarily on the state and local levels. Still others work for schools, hospitals, clinics, and other health facilities. A small but growing number of social workers are employed in business and industry.

COURSE REQUIREMENTS

Casework
Child Services
Child Welfare Services
Families at Risk
Family Health Care
Group Work
Human Behavior
Leadership and Group Action
Personality and Society
Psychology

Public Welfare
Social Legislation
Social Psychology
Social Services
Social Services for the Aging
Social Welfare Policy
Social Work
Social Work Processes
Systems Theory
Therapeutic Communications

OPTIONS WITHIN MAJOR

Community Mental Health
Counseling

Judicial Systems
Welfare Systems

RECOMMENDED HIGH SCHOOL COURSES

Biology
English
Psychology

Public Speaking
Sociology

The Career Connection for College Education

CAREERS	D.O.T. NUMBER	OUTLOOK	AVERAGE INITIAL SALARY
Associate Degree			
Social Service Assistant	195.367-034	Fair	$15,000
Bachelor Degrees			
Community Organization Worker	195.167-010	Fair	19,500
Delinquency Caseworker	195.107-026	Fair	19,000
Drug Control Officer	195.167-042	Fair	20,400
Parole Officer	195.107.046	Fair/Good	25,700
Probation Officer	195.107.046	Good	25,700
Social Caseworker	195.107-010	Good	20,100
Social Group Worker	195.107-022	Fair	20,100
Welfare Officer	195.117-010	Good	20,100
Graduate Degrees			
Certified Social Worker (ASCW)	195.107-034	Good	25,000
Graduate Social Worker (MSW)	195.105-030	Good/Exc.	23,500
Medical Social Worker	195.107-030	Fair	25,000
Professor	090.227-010	Good	32,900
Psychiatric Social Worker	195.107-034	Good	29,500
School Social Worker	195.107-038	Good	22,900
Social Worker Fellow (DSW)	195.107-030	Good/Exc.	31,000

Occupational Personality Styles: Serving, Social, Scientific

DPT Functions: Data = H   People = H   Things = L

GOE Work Groups: Social Research, Social Services

Sociology

Sociology is the study of human group behavior and interaction within families, communities, formal organizations, and societies. Sociologists study the social institutions formed by mankind and the influence which these institutions have upon the individual. Most sociologists are employed by universities and colleges, teaching and conducting research, but there are also opportunities in industry, organizations, and some secondary schools.

COURSE REQUIREMENTS

Applied Sociology
Collective Behavior
Deviance and Social Control
Juvenile Delinquency
Medical Sociology
Mental Health Services
Methods of Research in
    Sociology
Social Change
Social Organization

Social Problems
Social Psychology
Social Statistics
Social Stratification
Sociological Analysis
Sociology
Sociology of the Family
Sport Sociology
World Populations

OPTIONS WITHIN MAJOR

Applied Sociology
General Sociology

Professional Sociology
Secondary Education

RECOMMENDED HIGH SCHOOL COURSES

English (4 years)
History
Math

Psychology
Sociology

CAREERS	D.O.T. NUMBER	OUTLOOK	AVERAGE INITIAL SALARY
Bachelor Degrees			
Administrative Assistant	169.167-010	Fair/Good	$17,000
Community Organization Worker	195.167-010	Fair	19,500
Delinquency Caseworker	195.107-026	Fair	19,000
Social Caseworker	195.107-010	Good	20,100
Teacher	091.227-010	Fair	19,500
Graduate Degrees			
Criminologist	054.067-014	Fair/Good	24,000
Industrial Sociologist	054.067-014	Good	26,100
Penologist	054.107-010	Fair	26,900
Professor/Researcher	090.227-010	Good	32,900
Rural Sociologist	054.067-014	Fair	23,000
Social Ecologist	054.067-014	Fair	25,100
Social Pathologist		Good	28,300
Sociologist	054.067-014	Excellent	28,000
Urban Sociologist	054.067-014	Excellent	28,000

Occupational Personality Styles:　　Scientific, Social, Serving

DPT Functions:　　Data = H　　People = M　　Things = L

GOE Work Groups:　　Social Research, Social Services

Spanish

Spanish is one of the major languages in the world, ranking fifth in the number of native speakers (second only to English in the western hemisphere). In high schools, Spanish is the most frequently studied foreign language, accounting for almost 40 percent of all foreign language students. Besides teaching, bilingual graduates are needed in all phases of life to serve the millions of Spanish-speaking Americans in the Southwest and other areas.

COURSE REQUIREMENTS

Composition	Literature
Conversation	Phonetics
Cultural Civilization	Spanish
Grammar	Translation

OPTIONS WITHIN MAJOR

Business	Interpretation/Translation
Education	

RECOMMENDED HIGH SCHOOL COURSES

Geography	Literature
History	Social Science
Humanities	Spanish

CAREERS	D.O.T. NUMBER	OUTLOOK	AVERAGE INITIAL SALARY
Bachelor Degrees			
Customs Official	168.267-022	Fair	$16,500
Foreign-Service Officer	188.117-106	Fair	24,000
Import/Export Agent	184.117-022	Good	25,100
Intelligence Expert	059.267-010	Good	25,200
Interpreter	137.267-014	Fair/Good	23,100
Language Researcher	059.067-014	Fair	25,900
Public Relations Specialist	165.167-014	Fair/Good	29,100
Scientific Writer	131.267-026	Good	26,500
Teacher	091.227-010	Poor	19,500
Translator	137.267-018	Good	20,000
Travel Agent	252.152-010	Good	17,200
Graduate Degrees			
Professor	090.227-010	Good	32,900
Scientific Linguist	059.067-014	Fair	30,000

Occupational Personality Styles: Scientific, Social

DPT Functions: Data = H   People = M   Things = L

GOE Work Groups: Business Administration, Business Management, Educational and Library Services, Security Services

Special Education

An increasing awareness of children with handicaps has influenced the development of programs that offer specific training for teachers. Special education programs in the public schools are designed to help students who are severely intellectually handicapped, severely learning disabled, severely emotionally handicapped, and the mildly learning handicapped to study in resource room environments. The special education program may be offered as an individual program or combined with a major in elementary education.

COURSE REQUIREMENTS

Assessing Learning Dysfunctions	Psychology
Behavior Development	Resource Teaching
Computers in Education	Severely Emotionally Disabled
Educational Psychology	Severely Intellectually Disabled
Exceptional Children in School	Severely Learning Disabled
Human Development	Teaching Math
Learning Disabilities	Teaching Reading
Learning Theory	Teaching Science

OPTIONS WITHIN MAJOR

Emotionally Disabled	Learning Disabled
Intellectually Disabled	Resource Teaching

RECOMMENDED HIGH SCHOOL COURSES

English	Natural Sciences
Math	Social Science

CAREERS	D.O.T. NUMBER	OUTLOOK	AVERAGE INITIAL SALARY
Bachelor Degrees			
Teacher of the Handicapped	094.224-014	Excellent	$19,500
Teacher of the Mentally Retarded	094.227-030	Excellent	19,500
Graduate Degrees			
Administrator	099.117-026	Fair	44,000
Professor	099.227-010	Excellent	32,900

Occupational Personality Styles: Serving, Social

DPT Functions: Data = H   People = H   Things = L

GOE Work Groups: Educational and Library Services, Social Research

Speech Pathology and Audiology

Speech pathologists and audiologists provide direct services for people who have a speech or hearing impairment. The speech pathologist works with children and adults who have speech, language, and voice disorders. The audiologist primarily assesses and treats hearing problems.

Nearly one-half of speech pathologists and audiologists work in public schools. Colleges and universities employ many in classrooms, clinics, and research centers. The rest work in hospitals, speech and hearing centers, government agencies, industry, and private practice.

COURSE REQUIREMENTS

Acoustics
Analysis of Speech Production
Audiology
Auditory Processes
Aural Rehabilitation
Biology
Child Psychology
Communicative Disorders
Disorders of Articulation
Language Abilities

Linguistics
Phonetics
Psychological Aspects of
    Communication
Remediation Communication
    Disorders
Semantics
Sociology
Speech Anatomy
Speech Physiology

OPTIONS WITHIN MAJOR

Clinical
Education

Research

RECOMMENDED HIGH SCHOOL COURSES

Anatomy
Biology
English (4 years)
Math (3 years)

Physiology
Psychology
Public Speaking

CAREERS	D.O.T. NUMBER	OUTLOOK	AVERAGE INITIAL SALARY
Graduate Degrees			
Audiologist	076.101-010	Good/Exc.	$24,300
Professor	090.227-010	Good/Exc.	32,900
Speech Pathologist	076.107-010	Good/Exc.	24,300

Occupational Personality Styles: Scientific, Technical

DPT Functions: Data = H   People = H   Things = H

GOE Work Groups: Laboratory Technology, Life Sciences

Statistics

The statistician is an applied mathematician who uses design and analysis, operations research, probability theory, and other statistical tools to make decisions and solve problems for social scientists, biologists, economists, business people, and others who conduct research and collect data. Federal and state agencies, large industrial firms, and pharmaceutical companies are major employers of statisticians in discovering possible election outcomes, optimal methods and products, optimal business location, and a variety of sampling schemes. Graduates also play a key role in the field of actuarial science.

COURSE REQUIREMENTS

Analytical Geometry/Calculus
Categorical Data
Data Analysis
Experimental Design
Mathematical Statistics
Nonparametric Methods
Operation Research
Probability

Quality Control
Regression Analysis
Statistical Methods
Statistics
Survey Sampling
Theory of Linear Models
Theory of Statistics

OPTIONS WITHIN MAJOR

Actuarial Sciences
Computer Service

Research
Statistics

RECOMMENDED HIGH SCHOOL COURSES

Biology
Chemistry
Computer Science

English (4 years)
Math (3 years)
Physics

CAREERS	D.O.T. NUMBER	OUTLOOK	AVERAGE INITIAL SALARY
Bachelor Degrees			
Actuary	020.167-010	Good/Exc.	$27,500
Computer Programmer	030.162-010	Excellent	24,100
Market/Operating Research Analyst	050.067-014	Good/Exc.	25,100
Quality Controller	012.167-054	Good	23,900
Systems Analyst	030.167-014	Excellent	28,000
Graduate Degrees			
Professor	090.227-010	Excellent	32,900
Research	199.267-034	Excellent	33,000
Statistician	020.067-022	Excellent	30,400
Systems Analyst	030.167-014	Excellent	33,100

Occupational Personality Styles: Scientific, Detail-oriented

DPT Functions: Data = H   People = H   Things = L

GOE Work Group: Mathematics and Statistics

Theater and Cinematic Arts

Theater and cinematic arts attempt to provide the public with entertainment to fulfill their aesthetic needs. Graduates receive training in costuming, set design, acting, directing, playwriting, musical theater, motion picture and TV production, children's drama, or theater arts education. Many positions in the drama and film industries are highly competitive and openings in education vary from area to area. Employment opportunities and starting salaries are based on training, experience, and ability.

COURSE REQUIREMENTS

Acting
Acting for Cinema/Stage
Art of Interpretation
Audiovisual Production
Child Drama
Cinematography
Costume Design
Criticism of Film Art
Dialects
Directing
Directing the One-Act Play
Directing Theory
Film Editing
Film Sound

Motion Picture Art
Music
Musical Theater
Playwriting
Puppetry
Stage Makeup
Storytelling
Technical Theater
Theater for Children
Theater History
Theater Management
Theatrical Design
Voice, Diction, and Interpretation

OPTIONS WITHIN MAJOR

Acting
Child Drama
Costume Design
Designer/Technician

Directing
Motion-Picture and TV Production
Playwriting
Theater Arts Education

RECOMMENDED HIGH SCHOOL COURSES

Drama   Literature
English (4 years)   Speech
Forensics

CAREERS	D.O.T. NUMBER	OUTLOOK	AVERAGE INITIAL SALARY
Associate Degrees			
Costume Specialist	346.374-010	Good	$19,000
Performance Specialist		Fair	17,500
Bachelor Degrees			
Actor	150.047-010	Fair	Varies
Director	150.067-010	Fair/Good	33,200
Drama Coach	150.027-010	Fair	24,200
Motion-Picture/TV Director	159.167-014	Fair	35,000
Playwright	131.067-038	Fair/Good	Varies
Teacher	150.027-014	Good	19,500
Technical Director	150.067-010	Good	28,000
Graduate Degree			
Professor	090.227-010	Fair	32,900

Occupational Personality Styles: Artistic, Social

DPT Functions: Data = H   People = H   Things = M

GOE Work Group: Performing Arts: Drama

Veterinary Medicine

The majority of veterinarians are general practitioners who diagnose, treat, and control disease and injury in animals. Practice ranges from veterinary hospitals and clinics to farms and ranches. Specialists in veterinary medicine generally treat pets and small animals, although some deal with cattle, poultry, horse, or sheep care. Many veterinarians perform research related to animal disease and also serve as inspectors for local and federal government agencies. Although the need for many more veterinarians exists, there are only 18 veterinary schools and competition for admission is keen.

COURSE REQUIREMENTS

Most students accepted to veterinary school have a bachelor's degree. Courses include the following:

Animal Parasitology	Fundamentals of Animal Breeding
Animal Husbandry	Genetics
Biochemistry	Invertebrate Zoology
Biology	Microbiology
Calculus	Organic Chemistry
College Algebra	Pathology
College Chemistry	Physics
Feeds and Feeding	Virology

Professional school courses are a continuation of those above but in more depth and with clinical experiences.

OPTIONS WITHIN MAJOR

Anatomy	Pharmacology
Bacteriology	Physiology
Laboratory Animal Care	Radiology
Parasitology	Virology
Pathology	

RECOMMENDED HIGH SCHOOL COURSES

Biology
Chemistry
English (4 years)

Math (3 years)
Physics
Physiology

CAREERS	D.O.T. NUMBER	OUTLOOK	AVERAGE INITIAL SALARY
Graduate Degrees			
Veterinarian	073.101-010	Excellent	$40,100
Veterinary Anatomist	073.061-014	Excellent	42,000
Veterinary Bacteriologist	073.061-018	Good	35,000
Veterinary Epidemiologist	073.061-022	Good	35,900
Veterinary Pathologist	073.061-030	Good	44,000
Veterinary Physiologist	073.061-038	Excellent	42,000
Veterinary Virologist	041.061-058	Fair	41,800

Occupational Personality Styles: Scientific, Serving, Technical

DPT Functions: Data = H People = H Things = H

GOE Work Groups: Laboratory Technology, Life Sciences, Medical Sciences, Managerial Work: Plants and Animals

Wildlife Management

Wildlife specialists are professionals concerned with protecting and controlling our natural resources of soil, water, plants, and animals for the purpose of maintaining desired numbers of animals in accordance with public interest and welfare.

Employment opportunities are found with the state and federal agencies, Peace Corps, forest industry, state forestry agencies, cities, counties, educational institutions, consultants and others. Also, private laboratories and numerous scientifically based foundations have wildlife specialists on their staffs. Some wildlife specialists operate shooting or hunting reserves, manage private clubs, or act as writers or photographers of outdoor subjects.

COURSE REQUIREMENTS

Algebra
Biology
Botany
Calculus
Chemistry
Ecology
Economics
Environmental Conservation
Fish and Wildlife Biology

Fishery and Biology Management
Mammalogy
Physics
Plant Classification
Public Relations
Public Speaking
Soil Science
Statistics

OPTIONS WITHIN MAJOR

Wildlife Administration

Wildlife Biology

RECOMMENDED HIGH SCHOOL COURSES

Biology
Chemistry
English (3 years)
History

Math (3 years)
Physics
Social Studies

CAREERS	D.O.T. NUMBER	OUTLOOK	AVERAGE INITIAL SALARY
Associate Degree			
Forestry Technician	452.364-010	Fair/Good	$15,100
Bachelor Degrees			
Conservation Officer	379.137-018	Poor	17,000
Forestry Administrator	040.167-010	Poor	26,000
Photographer	143.062-030	Good	21,800
Wildlife Biologist	041.061-030	Fair	23,100
Wildlife Manager	379.167-018	Fair	25,000
Graduate Degree			
Professor	090.227-010	Fair	32,900

Occupational Personality Styles: Technical, Scientific, Serving

DPT Functions: Data = H   People = L   Things = H

GOE Work Groups: Life Sciences, Managerial Work: Plants and Animals

Youth Leadership

As the strength of the American home diminishes, the need for qualified leaders to work with youth increases. Youth leadership prepares such leaders to work in agencies such as the Boy Scouts of America, YMCA, YWCA, Boys Club of America, Camp Fire Girls, Girl Scouts, 4-H, Junior Achievement, and any other organization that serves the youth. The outdoor-education program in survival and other pioneering programs require skilled development and direction as they seek to positively change behavior. Aside from professional training, students are prepared to assist community and church volunteer programs.

COURSE REQUIREMENTS

Camp Administration
Camp Counseling
Career Internship
Career Observations
Community Relationships
Executive Dynamics
Executive Field Training
  Seminar
Finance

First-aid/Emergency Care
Intramural Sports
Introduction to Youth Leadership
Keys to Leadership
Moving Camps
Outdoor Leadership
Practicum
Trail Leadership

OPTIONS WITHIN MAJOR

Agency Emphasis

Outdoor-Education Emphasis

RECOMMENDED HIGH SCHOOL COURSES

Biological Sciences
Communications
English (3 years)

Extracurricular Activities
Speech

CAREERS	D.O.T. NUMBER	OUTLOOK	AVERAGE INITIAL SALARY
Bachelor Degrees			
Boy Scout Professional	153.117-018	Fair	$21,500
County Extension Agent	096.127-014	Fair	20,000
Field Staff Executive	189.267-010	Fair	21,500
Training Director	166.167-026	Fair	20,000
Youth Agency Admin.	096.127-022	Good	21,500

Occupational Personality Styles: Serving, Social, Influencing

DPT Functions: Data = H   People = H   Things = M

GOE Work Groups: Hospitality Services, Services Administration, Social Services

Zoology

Zoologists deal with all aspects of animal life (including man) on submicroscopic, microscopic, and macroscopic levels. Zoologists must become familiar with knowledge and techniques of chemistry, physics, math, and several types of laboratories. With this broad background, zoologists serve as laboratory and X-ray technicians, dental hygienists, and pharmaceutical lab specialists, as well as in government, private research, and business. Many preprofessional students of dentistry, medicine, and other health services major in zoology.

COURSE REQUIREMENTS

Animal Systemics
Aquaculture
Bioethics
Cell and Developmental Biology
Ecology
Embryology
Entomology
Environmental Biology
Evolution Theory
Genetics
Heredity and Reproduction
Herpetology
Histology
Human Anatomy
Human Physiology

Ichthyology
Insect Morphology
Insects
Invertebrate Zoology
Mammalogy
Marine Biology
Medical Parasitology
Microbiology
Organic Chemistry
Ornithology
Physiology
Plant Science
Vertebrate Zoology
Zoology

OPTIONS WITHIN MAJOR

Applied Zoology
Education

Preprofessional
Research

The Career Connection for College Education

RECOMMENDED HIGH SCHOOL COURSES

Biology   English
Chemistry   Math

CAREERS	D.O.T. NUMBER	OUTLOOK	AVERAGE INITIAL SALARY
Bachelor Degrees			
Biologist	041.676-030	Fair	$23,500
Park Naturalist	049.127-010	Fair/Good	19,500
Teacher	091.227-010	Good	19,500
Wildlife Biologist	041.061-030	Fair/Good	23,100
Wildlife Manager	379.167-018	Poor	25,000
Zoologist	041.061-090	Fair/Good	23,600
Graduate Degrees			
Animal Physiologist	041.061-078	Fair/Good	25,100
Aquatic Biologist	041.061-022	Fair	25,100
Biologist	041.061-030	Good	27,800
Biophysicist	041.061-034	Good	33,400
Cytologist	041.061-042	Fair	28,000
Entomologist	041.061-046	Good	29,000
Geneticist	041.061-050	Good	24,600
Histopathologist	041.061-054	Excellent	29,000
Professor	090.227-010	Good	32,900
Zoologist	041.061-090	Good/Exc.	32,000

Occupational Personality Styles: Scientific, Technical

DPT Functions: Data = H   People = L   Things = H

GOE Work Groups: Laboratory Technology, Life Sciences, Managerial Work: Plants and Animals

Auxiliary Information

There is a definite relationship between the type and level of education one pursues and career choices. When one makes plans for education or careers it is more helpful to begin with the end in mind. The following questions may be important to ask:

1. What career do I want?
2. Will the job that I want today be the one I want 20 years from now?
3. How far do I want to go in education or training?
4. What type of education or training will I be happiest in pursuing?
5. Will my intended educational plans help me get the job I want?
6. If I begin my education along one path and change, what effect will it have?

As you study the alternatives on the accompanying chart, remember these important points:

1. There are several ways to become trained and educated.
2. There are several careers available in each occupational field.
3. To enter certain jobs, you must have certain levels of education.
4. Generally speaking, the more training or education you have, the higher the number of available jobs.
5. You can change your mind about the level or type of training, but it is easier and less time-consuming to begin on the right track.

ALTERNATIVES FOR POST-HIGH SCHOOL EDUCATION

Specialized School

Short-term (6 to 24 months), specialized training in a technical area is provided by this type of school. Very few "non-essential" classes are required. Quite often a technical school provides only one area of emphasis, such as dental technology, cosmetology, business, etc.

Technical College

Here, general education courses are mixed with technical training. A technical college may offer associate degrees that transfer to a four-year college or university. More often, programs are terminal in nature, preparing students for careers upon completion.

Two-year Community College

These are also called junior colleges. While short-term degrees are offered, most students attend these schools in preparation for four-year colleges or universities. You can earn an associate degree in two years or transfer any time after the first enrollment.

Four-year College

An associate degree or bachelor degree can be earned at this level of higher education. Some four-year colleges also offer limited graduate degrees. A wide variety of courses are available.

University

A university provides a great variety of course work and several levels of degrees. A university is divided into several "colleges," such as the College of Business or the College of Biological Sciences. Degrees range from associate, bachelor, master, and doctoral programs. Each college is composed of several departments. A department may offer one or more majors.

Transfer of Credit

Students often accumulate credit at one school then transfer to another one in order to complete a degree. If courses are college-level courses, the credit will transfer from one accredited institution to another. When a student transfers to a new school, official transcripts of all credits must be sent from all previous institutions to the admissions office of the new institution.

GRADUATION REQUIREMENTS

Credit Hour

Credit is awarded for courses based on the amount of time spent in class per week. For example, a five-credit course generally requires one to be in class five periods each week. A two-hour class requires two class periods per week. Often a laboratory period is extra at a technical school or a technical college. An average load is 14–17 quarter or semester hours for each registration.

Quarter Hour

In a quarter system, the year is divided into four parts. One academic year equals three quarters.

Semester Hour

There are three semesters in one year. One academic year equals two semesters.

Transfer

When you transfer from a quarter system to a semester system it may appear that you lose credits. Just remember that there are three quarters but only two semesters in each academic year. Therefore, three quarter hours credit equals two semester hours credit.

Graduation

This denotes an academic accomplishment that has been outlined by the school. Basic requirements usually include:

1. general education courses
2. courses in a major field of study
3. a minimum number of credit hours
4. passing specifically required examinations or courses.

Degrees

Various degrees are awarded by schools. The first three are usually obtained at technical schools, technical colleges, or specialty schools.

Types of Degrees

1. **Certificate:** a six- to twelve-month course
2. **Junior college degree:** a one-year course
3. **Associate degree of Applied Science or Arts:** a two-year degree that usually does not transfer all credits to a college or university
4. **Associate of Arts or Science:** a two-year degree used for job preparation or transferring
5. **Bachelor of Arts or Science:** a four-year degree
6. **Master of Arts or Science, Engineering, Business, etc.:** a one- to two-year course beyond the bachelor level
7. **Doctor of Education, Philosophy, Medicine, etc.:** a two- to four-year course beyond the master level

General Education

Breadth of knowledge is at least as important as depth of knowledge. To ensure that students are well educated, technical schools require students to take a number of classes in a variety of areas.

Major

When a student decides the specialty desired, a major is selected. The courses are usually sequential, starting with the simple and moving to the more complex.

Getting admitted to a college of your choice takes time and effective planning. Often, what you have accomplished as early as the ninth grade will impact your chances for admissions. The closer you get to graduation, the more important it will become to know clearly the steps that will help. Your counselors are an indispensable part of your admissions efforts. They are in contact with college representatives and have both experience and information that will be helpful. Below is a sequence that can become meaningful to you. It is followed by a description of each step.

---

1 TAKE COLLEGE PREP CLASSES

2 WORK HARD IN CLASSES

3 TAKE COLLEGE ADMISSIONS TESTS

4 APPLY FOR ADMISSIONS

5 SELECT A COLLEGE

6 IMPLEMENT YOUR PLAN

Take College Prep Classes

Beginning with the ninth grade, the specific high school courses that you choose will be important in your admission to college. Most colleges, especially those universities that cannot accept all the applicants that apply, have outlined specific courses that are designated *college prep*. A rule of thumb is that if a class is both required for graduation and is an academically oriented course, it is considered college prep. Examples would be U.S. History, Algebra II, foreign languages, and laboratory sciences. Be careful, because classes such as journalism and psychology are often thought to be college prep by students, but not by admissions committees who evaluate high school transcripts.

Selective colleges and universities request that from 50% to 70% of your classes in high school be college prep. Avoid the reasoning that you will build your grades by taking non-college prep courses. On the other hand, look for the opportunity to take honors and especially advanced placement courses. How serious a student is about higher education is often reflected in the types of classes taken.

Work Hard in the Classes

Grades and grade point averages are calculated, for admissions decisions, from the ninth through the twelfth grades. Typically an "A" = 4 points, "B" = 3 points, "C" = 2 points, and "D" = 1 point. You can calculate your cumulative grade point average by (1) multiplying the units (for example, hours) of each class times the points earned for the grade of the class—this is called the grade point, (2) add up the total units for all the classes, (3) add the grade points for all the classes, and (4) divide the total grade points by the total number of units.

Most colleges look at the total or cumulative grade point average (GPA) for all your classes. However, there are some college and universities that are highly selective that also want the GPA for college prep courses. Although not common, in these colleges with highly selective admissions, higher weighted points are given for honors and advanced placement courses (that is, an "A" might equal more than 4 points, etc.). You will need to check with the particular college for which you have an interest to know their policies.

Take the College Admissions Tests

The two most frequently given college entrance tests are the Scholastic Aptitude Test (SAT) and the American College Test (ACT). Colleges usually have a preference for the test they want you to take. Both tests are given on specific dates at a specific place. Approximately six weeks is required between the time you apply for the test and the date you will take it. If you do not apply on time, the testing companies will not send a test for you.

The SAT has verbal and numerical sections. The ACT tests in English, math, social science, and natural science. You will be compared against all other students who take the test in the nation, your state, and your school. When colleges receive the results of your tests, your score will be compared to students in that school.

A large controversy exists as to whether you can prepare for the tests. Studies have resulted in conflicting findings. It is, however, to your advantage to become familiar with the types of questions you will be encountering on the tests. Your counselor will be able to help you with booklets provided from the testing company.

Apply for Admissions

Before applying for admissions to a college, find out about their admissions policies. For example, there are three types of admissions. Colleges with an *open* admissions policy require a high school diploma or its equivalent and typically have a minimum age factor. Many colleges have a *selective* admissions policy, which requires specific information such as GPA and college entrance examination scores. These colleges have established minimum requirements regarding grades and test results that are necessary for a student to attain. A third category includes those colleges (typically large universities that have graduate programs and conduct research) that have a *highly selective* policy for admissions. They also require GPA and test scores, but they often require other information such as percent of your high school courses that are college prep, GPA on your college prep courses, letters of recommendation, an essay from you to identify your educational goals and to test your writing ability, interviews, and a record of extracurricular activities. If the college is sponsored by a church, an endorsement from your ecclesiastical leader may be requested.

When letters of recommendation are requested, understand that the college is interested in knowing how well you can do academically. Therefore, avoid the temptation of having a friend, community leader, or neighbor write a letter elaborating on other than educational endeavors. Those letters that have the most influence are from teachers of strong academic courses.

Students are sometimes disappointed when they fail to get their application completed and to the college before the deadline. Most colleges have deadlines, and those with selective or highly selective admissions policies hold strictly to that deadline.

Your counselor typically has copies of catalogs of local institutions and those where many of the students in your school have traditionally enrolled. If they are not readily available, the counselor can help you find where to write for catalogs and application materials.

Select a College

When selecting a college there are several factors to consider. One of the first is finances. Limited finances may suggest that you attend a college while living at home. Costs of housing and food are often expensive. The cost of tuition also influences finances. Work with your counselor to identify all the costs that you will incur at the colleges you are considering. Compare the costs to your financial resources.

Another important factor to consider is whether the college has the academic major that you want to study. If you have not chosen a major, this may not be a significant determinant. However, if you are considering a major such as nursing or engineering, it is important to begin at the college from which you want to graduate. The reason is that courses in these programs are highly sequential and begin the first semester that you enroll. If you miss the first sequence, you may have to wait a complete year for the sequence to begin again. Because the number of majors that are very structured is increasing, it is usually a good practice to start at the school from which you want to get your degree.

If you plan to attend a community college in order to take your general education courses and then transfer to a four-year college or university, select your courses carefully. While all college-level courses transfer from one accredited institution to another, they may not fit into the category you intended. For example, a class that is considered a general education course in physical science at a community college may not be classified as the same in a particular four-year college. It will transfer as an elective, but not in the area you intended. The same is also true for classes in one's major. Most community colleges have lists of their courses and how they transfer to specific local institutions. Acquire those lists and select your courses with your transfer in mind.

Other considerations are important in selecting a college. A few are distance from home, size of the student body, athletic or fine arts programs, and work opportunities. Take time and carefully consider your choice. College is costly in both time and money.

Implement Your Plan

The time between your application for admissions and when you go to school is important. Here are a few things to consider.

When you apply for admission, the application will usually ask for the major you intend to pursue. Even if you are not certain, select a major that you are considering and list it. Most colleges will send you valuable information about that particular major, which will include the courses they recommend for your first enrollment period.

Check on housing and make the necessary arrangements early to increase the probability of getting a desired roommate or living in an area of your liking. If a job is necessary for you, find out how to apply for on-campus jobs and locate off-campus possibilities; begin aggressively pursuing potential opportunities. Contact the financial aid office early and continue this association until you are satisfied that you have your financial aid package firmly in place.

THE ANATOMY OF A JOB

There are many aspects of a particular job that are important to consider when making career choices. Following is a brief outline of the major components. Remember that decisions are enhanced or inhibited by the accuracy of the information and perception you have about a particular job. One of the most helpful steps in making your decisions is to fantasize yourself in the job—working in the environment, doing the tasks, being with the people. Ask yourself when doing this very productive daydreaming: "Am I comfortable in this situation? Can I do what is necessary?"

Working Conditions

Based on periodic job analysis, these may change from place to place and as different phenomenon occur.

1. Indoor/outdoor work environment
2. Indoor temperature changes and ranges

3. Humidity ranges and changes

4. Noise and vibration

5. Hazards

6. Fumes, odors, toxic conditions, dust, and ventilation

Tasks or Duties

Not only are the specific tasks important to know, but the types of tasks offer you the opportunity to express yourself.

1. Working primarily with data, people, or things

2. The relationship of work with these three elements

General Nature and Description

This component is strongly related to the type of lifestyle you can live as a result of your particular job.

1. Hours—shift or regular

2. Physical or mental exertion

3. Flexible, creative, or routine work

4. Individual or teamwork atmosphere

5. Work for self or supervisor

6. Salaried or time card

7. Travel or stationary

8. Extracurricular requirements

Places of Employment

Geography is often one of the single most influential factors in a career choice. People will often compromise other factors to live in a particular area.

1. Size of organization

2. Location—urban/rural

3. Organizational structure

4. Public/private

Outlook

Outlook refers to both the availability of jobs at job entry and the longevity of that job and related horizontal or lateral opportunities.

Entry:	**Longevity:**
Availability	Opportunities for advancement
Competition	Projected forecast of industry
Locations	turnover rate
Obligations	Physical considerations—
Union memberships	Pregnancy
	Additional training needs
	Tenure date

Salary and Benefits

While the initial salary is important, perhaps a greater impact on your financial life will be the projected increases. These future increases are more dependent on the amount of education you have than initial salaries.

1. Entry level
2. Rate of inflation increases
3. Mode of payment—overtime, salary, piecework, or commission
4. Projected ceilings
5. Bonuses
6. Rate-of-pay increases
7. Medical benefits
8. Profit sharing
9. Stock options
10. Educational benefits
11. Travel
12. Discounts
13. Physical fitness opportunities
14. Retirement
15. Housing
16. Cost-of-living adjustments
17. Child care
18. Union benefits

Indexes

Index of Majors

Listed below are major areas of study along with the corresponding page numbers for more detailed information about that major.

Accounting, 26
Advertising, 28
Aerospace and aeronautical
    engineering, 30
African studies, 32
Agricultural economics, 34
Agronomy, 36
American studies, 38
Animal science, 40
Anthropology, 42
Architecture, 44
Art, 46
Asian studies, 48
Botany, 50
Business education, 52
Business management, 54
Canadian studies, 56
Chemical engineering, 58
Chemistry, 60
Chinese, 62
Civil engineering, 64
Classical languages, 66
Clothing and textiles, 68
Commercial art, design
    and photography, 70
Communications, 72
Community health education, 74
Computer science, 76
Dance and physical education, 78
Dentistry, 80
Design and illustration, 82
Design engineering technology, 84
Dietetics, 86
Drafting, 88
Early childhood education, 90

Economics, 92
Educational psychology, 94
Electrical engineering, 96
Electronics engineering
    technology, 98
Elementary education, 100
English, 102
Environmental health, 104
European studies, 106
Family resource management, 108
Finance and banking, 110
Food science, 112
Forestry, 114
French, 116
Genealogy, 118
Geography, 120
Geology, 122
Geophysics, 124
German, 126
Health administration, 128
Health science, 130
History, 132
Home economics education, 134
Horticulture, 136
Hotel management, 138
Industrial administration, 140
Industrial education, 142
Information management, 144
Insurance, 146
Japanese, 148
Journalism, 150
Landscape architecture, 152
Latin American studies, 154
Law, 156
Library science, 158

Linguistics, 160

Manufacturing engineering
technology, 162

Marketing and retailing, 164

Mathematics, 166

Mechanical engineering, 168

Medical technology, 170

Medicine, 172

Metallurgical engineering, 174

Microbiology, 176

Mining and geological
engineering, 178

Music, 180

Near Eastern studies, 182

Nursing, 184

Occupational health and safety, 186

Occupational therapy, 188

Oceanography, 190

Optometry, 192

Pharmacy, 194

Philosophy, 196

Physical education, 198

Physical therapy, 200

Physics and astronomy, 202

Political science, 204

Portuguese, 206

Psychology, 208

Public administration, 210

Public relations, 212

Range management, 214

Recreation management, 216

Russian, 218

Secondary education, 220

Social work, 222

Sociology, 224

Spanish, 226

Special education, 228

Speech pathology and
audiology, 230

Statistics, 232

Theater and cinematic arts, 234

Veterinary medicine, 236

Wildlife management, 238

Youth leadership, 240

Zoology, 242

Index of Careers

The courses covered in this book are listed below, along with the page numbers where additional information can be found.

Account executive, 29
Accountant, 27
  budget and forecast, 27
  cost, 27
  general, 27
  property, 27
  tax, 27
Acquisition librarian, 159
Actor, 235
Actuary, 147, 167, 233
Acupuncturist, 173
Administration/management engineer, 97
Administrative assistant, 53, 145, 225
Administrative dietitian, 87
Administrator, educational, 101
Administrator, numerous
Advertising designer, 47, 83
Advertising manager, 29, 73
Aerodynamicist, 31
Aeronautical-design engineer, 31
Aeronautical drafter, 89
Aeronautical engineer, 31
Aeronautical-research engineer, 31
Aeronautical stress analyst, 31
Aeronautical-test engineer, 31
Agribusiness management, 35
Agribusiness technologist, 35
Agricultural agent, 35, 37
Agricultural appraiser, 35, 215
Agricultural economist, 35
Agricultural engineer, 37
Agricultural supplier, 35
Agronomist, 37

Airport engineer, 65
Airport manager, 55, 211
Allergist, 173
Anesthesiologist, 173
Animal physiologist, 243
Animal scientist, 41
Anthropologist, 43, 67
  applied, 43
  cultural, 43
  physical or social, 43
Applications engineer, 97
Aquatic biologist, 243
Archaeological technician, 43
Archaeologist, 43, 67
Architect, 45
  landscape, 153
  marine, 45
  urban planner, 45
Architectural drafter, 85, 89
Archivist, 43, 67, 133, 159
Arranger of music, 181
Art director, 29, 47
Artist
  commercial, 29, 83
  copy, 29, 47, 83
  fashion, 47, 71, 83
  graphic, 71, 83
  quick sketch, 47
  studio, 47
Art therapist, 47
Assayer, 61
Assistant manager, numerous
Assistant vice-president, numerous
Astronomer, 203
Astrophysicist, 203

Athletic director, 199
Athletic manager, college, 199
Athletic trainer, 199
Audiologist, 231
Audiovisual librarian, 159
Audiovisual production
   specialist, 47
Audiovisual specialist, 101
Auditor, 27, 167
Automotive design drafter, 89
Automotive engineer, 169

Bank examiner, 27
Banker, 55
Bar examiner, 157
Biochemist, 61
Biographer, 33, 39, 49, 57, 107, 133,
   155, 183
Biologist, 243
Biologist, aquatic, 243
Biologist, marine, 191
Biomedical engineer, 59
Biophysicist, 203, 243
Blind, therapist for, 95
Book editor, 103
Botanist, 51
Boy scout professional, 217, 241
Broker, 55, 111
Budget/management
   analyst, 55, 211
Building construction
   supervisor, 141
Bursar, 27
Business consultant, 53, 157
Business manager, numerous
Business market research
   analyst, 93
Business programmer, 77
Buyer, 55, 69, 165, 211

Cardiologist, 173
Career assessment officer, 95
Career counselor, 95
Cartographer, 121
Cartographic drafter, 89
Cartoonist, 47

Castings drafter, 89
Cataloger, 159
Cattle rancher, 41
Certified social worker, 223
Chemical design engineer, 59
Chemical engineer, 59
Chemical engineer technician, 59
Chemical equipment engineer, 59
Chemical laboratory chief, 61
Chemical lab technician, 61
Chemical metallurgist, 175
Chemical operator, 59, 61
Chemical physicist, 203
Chemical technologist, 61
Chemist, 61
Chief executive officer, numerous
Chief executive officer or
   president, 111
Chief petroleum engineer, 179
Choreographer, 79
Civil drafter, 89
Civil engineer, 65
Civil engineering technician, 65
Claims adjuster, 35, 147
Claims examiner, 147
Classifier, 159
Clergy, 197
Clerk-typist, 145
Climatologist, 121
Clinical dietitian, 87
Clinical psychologist, 209
Cloth designer, 71
Clothes designer, 69
Coach, drama, 235
Coach, high school, 199
Columnist, 151, 205
Commercial artist, 29, 83
Commercial designer, 71, 83
Communications engineer, 97, 99
Communications technologist, 99
Community health planner, 75, 105
Community health
   representative, 75
Community organization
   officer, 209

Community organization
  worker, 223, 225
Composer, 181
Computer-aided designer, 85
Computer-aided drafter, 85
Computer-aided manufacturing
  consultant, 163
Computer applications
  engr., 77, 167
Computer designer, 99
Computer operator, 77
Computer programmer, 77, 233
Computer systems engineer, 77
Computer technologist, 99
Computer translator, 161
Conductor, 181
Conservation officer, 239
Construction engineer, 65
Construction inspector, 141
Construction supervisor, 169
Consultant, numerous
Consultant/researcher, 43
Consulting engineer, 97
Consumer affairs staff, 109
Controller, 27, 111
Copy artist, 29, 47, 83
Copywriter, 73, 103
Corporate lawyer, 157
Correspondent, 33, 39, 49, 57, 107,
  151, 155, 183, 205
Cost accountant, 27
Costume specialist, 235
Counseling, director, 95
Counseling psychologist, 95, 209
Counselor, 95, 189
  career, 95
  employment, 209
  family financial planning, 109
  mental health, 95
  school, 95
  state rehabilitation, 95
  substance abuse, 95
County extension agent, 241
Credit manager, 55
Criminal lawyer, 157
Criminologist, 61, 225

Critic, 103, 197
Cultural anthropologist, 43
Customs official, 63, 117, 127, 149,
  207, 219, 227
Cytologist, 177, 243
Cytotechnologist, 171, 177

Dairy manager, 41
Dairy scientist, 41
Dairy technologist, 41
Dance performer, 79
Dance teacher, 79
Data typist, 145
Day care center worker, 91
Delinquency caseworker, 223, 225
Dental technologist, 171
Dentist, 81
Department editor, 151
Department supervisor,
  numerous
Dermatologist, 173
Design drafter, 89
Design engineer, 85, 97, 169
Design engineer, aeronautical, 31
Designer
  advertising, 47, 83
  cloth, 71
  commercial, 71, 83
  computer, 99
  computer-aided, 85
  die, 163
  environmental, 153
  fashion, 69
  furniture, 47
  graphic, 71
  industrial, 71, 85, 169
  interior, 71
  layout, 47, 83
  set, 47
  theater costume, 69
  tool, 163
Development and research
  engineer, 97
Dialysis technician, 171
Die designer, 163

Dietetic educator, 87
Dietitian, 113
Dietitian, administrative, 87
Dietitian, research, 87
Directional drafter, 89
Director, counseling, 95
Director, guidance, 95
Director, numerous
Director of transportation, 55, 211
District attorney, 157
Doctor, *See* Medical doctor
Drafter, 45, 89
  aeronautical, 89
  architectural, 85, 89
  automotive design, 89
  cartographic, 89
  castings, 89
  civil, 89
  computer-aided, 85
  design, 89
  directional, 89
  electrical, 89
  electronics, 89
  geological, 89
  mechanical, 89
  patent, 89
  structural, 89
  tool design, 89
  topographical, 89
Drama coach, 235
Drug control officer, 223

Ecologist, forest, 115
Economist, 93
Editor, 73, 103
  book, 103
  department, 151
  editorial writer, 137, 197
  journalist, 133
  magazine, 137
  managing, 151
  newspaper, 103, 151
  publications, 33, 39, 49, 57, 103,
    107, 155, 183
  story, 103
  technical scientific, 103

Editorial writer, 137, 197
Educational administrator, 101, 221
Educational psychologist, 95, 209
Efficiency engineer, 167
Electrical drafter, 89
Electrical engineer, 97
Electrical power technician, 99
Electrical test engineer, 97
Electrocardiographic technician,
  171
Electroencephalographic
  technician, 171
Electro-optical engineer, 97, 203
Electronic physicist, 203
Electronics drafter, 89
Electronics engineer, 97, 99
Electronics system manager, 99
Electronics system specialist, 99
Electronics technician, 99
Electronics test engineer, 97, 99
Elementary teacher, 47, 91
Employment counselor, 209
Engineer, 169
  administration/mgt., 97
  aeronautical, 31
  aeronautical-design, 31
  aeronautical-research, 31
  aeronautical-test engineer, 31
  agricultural, 37
  airport, 65
  applications, 97
  automotive, 169
  biomedical, 59
  chemical, 59
  chemical design, 59
  chemical equipment, 59
  chief petroleum, 179
  civil, 65
  communications, 97, 99
  computer applications, 77, 167
  computer systems, 77
  construction, 65
  consulting, 97
  design, 85, 97, 169
  development and research,
    numerous

The Career Connection for College Education

efficiency, 167
electrical, 97
electrical test, 97
electronics, 97, 99
electronics test, 97, 99
electro-optical, 97, 203
geological mining, 123
groundwater, 123
highway, 65
hydraulic, 65
industrial, 163
industrial health, 187
irrigation, 65
manufacturing, 163
mechanical, 169
mining, 179
mining, geological, 123
nuclear, 59
oceanographic, 191
petroleum, 59
petroleum geologist, 123
plant, 141
power, solid-state, 97
project, 163
quality control, 163
research, 97
sanitation, 65
structural, 65
systems, 77, 97
transportation, 65
Engineering assistant, 85
Engineering professor, 97
Engineering psychologist, 209
Engineering researcher, numerous
Engineering technician, 89
English as a second language
    instructor, 161
Entomologist, 243
Environmental designer, 153
Environmental health
    scientist, 59, 105, 177
Environmental health
    specialist, 105, 187
Environmental researcher, 121
Estate planner, 109, 111

Ethnologist, 43
Executive director, numerous
Executive secretary, 145
Exercise physiologist, 199
Exercise specialist, 199
Experimental psychologist, 209
Extension service specialist, 35, 69,
    109, 135
Extractive metallurgist, 175

Family financial planning and
    counseling, 109
Family practitioner, 173
Family/social services staff, 109
Farm management adviser, 35
Farm manager, 35, 215
Farm real estate salesperson, 35
Fashion artist, 47, 71, 83
Fashion coordinator, 69
Fashion designer, 69
Fashion illustrator, 69
Fashion promoter, 69
Federal meat grader, 41
Field staff executive, 241
Field supervisor, 141
Financial aid officer, 111
Financial analyst, 111
Florist, 137
Food and drug inspector, 105
Food and meat inspector, 41
Food chemist, 113
Food retailer distributor, 35
Food scientist, 113
Food service agent, 35
Food services director, 139
Food systems management, 113
Food technologist, 105, 113
Foreign-service officer, 33, 39, 49,
    57, 63, 107, 117, 127, 133, 149,
    155, 183, 205, 207, 219, 227
Forest ecologist, 115
Forest ranger, 115
Forester, 115
Forestry administrator, 239
Forestry technician, 115, 239

Fund-raiser, 213
Furniture designer, 47

Genealogist, 67, 133
Genealogy research specialist, 119
General accountant, 27
General practitioner, 173
General research, numerous
Geneticist, 41, 51, 243
Geodesist, 123, 125
Geographer, 121, 191
Geological drafter, 89
Geological mining engineer, 123
Geologist, 123
Geologist, marine, 191
Geologist, petroleum engineer, 123
Geophysical drafter, 89
Geophysicist, 123, 125, 203
Government economist, 93
Government worker, numerous
Graduate social worker, 223
Graphic artist, 71, 83
Graphic designer, 71
Groundwater engineer, 123
Guidance director, 95
Gynecologist, 173

Handicapped, teacher of, 229
Health and safety inspector, 105
Health care center worker, 75
Health care inspector, 105
Health care officer, 131
Health organization worker, 75
Health physicist, 203
Health scientist, 131
Health services adviser, 75, 131
Health teacher, 131
Highway engineer, 65
Histopathologist, 243
Historian, 33, 39, 49, 57, 67, 107, 133, 155, 183
Historical society director, 133
Home economics teacher, 135
Home economist, 135
Horticultural researcher, 137

Horticulturist, 137
Hospital administrator, 129
Hospital lab education administrator, 171
Hospital or health service coordinator, 171
Hotel/motel clerk, 139
Hotel recreation manager, 139, 217
Hotel and restaurant administrator, 139, 217
Human performance researcher, 131
Hydraulic engineer, 65
Hydrologist, 123, 125
Hygienist, industrial, 131, 187

Illustrator, 47, 71, 83
Import/export agent, 33, 39, 49, 57, 63, 107, 117, 127, 149, 155, 183, 207, 219, 227
Industrial arts teacher, 143
Industrial designer, 71, 85, 169
Industrial engineer, 163
Industrial engineer technician, 85
Industrial health engineer, 187
Industrial hygienist, 105, 131, 187
Industrial laboratory technician, 163
Industrial location geographer, 121
Industrial nurse, 185
Industrial psychologist, 209
Industrial psychometrist, 209
Industrial recreation director, 217
Industrial sociologist, 225
Industrial therapist, 209
Information systems programmer, 77
Insurance lawyer, 157
Insurance underwriter, 147
Intelligence expert, 33, 39, 49, 57, 63, 67, 107, 117, 127, 149, 155, 161, 183, 207, 219, 227
Interior designer, 71
Internal revenue service agent, IRS, 55

Internist, 173
Interpreter, 63, 117, 127, 149, 207, 219, 227
Intramural sports director, 199
Irrigation engineer, 65

Job analyst, 55, 165
Journalist, 73, 151
Journalist/editor, 133
Judge, 157
Junior officer, numerous

Kindergarten teacher, 91

Labor relations manager, 55
Laboratory tester, 59, 61
Land-use planner, 123
Land/water use analyst, 37
Landscape architect, 137, 153
Landscape contractor/estimator, 137, 153
Language researcher, 63, 117, 127, 149, 207, 219, 227
Law enforcement trainee, 205
Lawyer, 157
    corporate, 157
    criminal, 157
    district attorney, 157
    insurance, 157
    patent, 157
    probate, 157
    real estate, 157
    tax attorney, 157
    title attorney, 157
Layout designer, 47, 83
Learning specialist, 95, 221
Legal secretary, 145
Librarian, 119, 133
Librarian, acquisition, 159
Librarian, audiovisual, 159
Librarian, reference, 159
Librarian, school, 159
Library technician, 159
Licensed practical nurse, 185
Linguist, 43

Linguist, scientific, 63, 67, 117, 127, 149, 161, 219, 227
Livestock extension agent, 41
Loan officer, 111
Lobbyist, 213

Management analyst, 55
Manager, numerous
Managing editor, 151
Manual arts therapist, 143, 209
Manufacturing engineer, 163
Map curator, 121
Marine architect, 45
Marine biologist, 191
Marine geologist, 191
Market/data analyst, 35
Market research analyst, 35, 55, 93, 165, 233
Marketing retail analyst, 165
Materials science technician, 163
Mathematician, 167
Meat grader, federal, 41
Mechanical drafter, 89
Mechanical engineer, 169
Media specialist, 159
Medical doctor
    acupuncturist, 173
    allergist, 173
    anesthesiologist, 173
    cardiologist, 173
    dermatologist, 173
    family practitioner, 173
    general practitioner, 173
    gynecologist, 173
    internist, 173
    neurologist, 173
    obstetrician, 173
    opthalmologist, 173
    orthopedic surgeon, 173
    pathologist, 173
    pediatrician, 173
    proctologist, 173
    psychiatrist, 173
    surgeon, 173
    urologist, 173

Medical facilities director, 129
Medical illustrator, 47
Medical laboratory technician, 171
Medical researcher, 171
Medical secretary, 145
Medical social worker, 223
Medical technologist, 171
Mental health counselor, 95
Mentally retarded, teacher of, 95, 229
Metallographer, 175
Metallurgical engineering technician, 175
Metallurgist
  chemical, 175
  extractive, 175
  physical, 175
Metals/materials technician, 175
Meteorologist, 203
Microbiologist, 177
Microbiology technologist, 177
Mineralogist, 123
Mining engineer, 179
Mining engineer technician, 179
Mining geologist/engineer, 123, 179
Motion-picture photographer, 73
Motion-picture/TV director, 73, 235
Municipal recreation
  administrator, 217
Museum curator, 43
Museum technician, 43
Music copyist, 181
Music director, instructor, 181
Music director, TV, 181
Music therapist, 181

Naturalist, park, 243
Navigator, 167
Nematologist, 51
Neurologist, 173
News analyst, 151
Newscaster, radio, 151
News editor, 151
Newspaper editor, 103, 151
Newswriter, 73

Nuclear engineer, 59
Nuclear medical technologist, 171
Nurse anesthetist, 185
Nurse instructor, 185
Nurse, licensed practical, 185
Nurse, midwife, 185
Nurse, public health, 185
Nurse, registered, 185
Nurse, supervisor, 185
Nursery school director, 91
Nutritionist, 75, 87
Nutritionist, public health, 185

Obstetrician, 173
Occupational safety inspector, 187
Occupational therapist, 189
Oceanographer, physical, 191
Oceanographic engineer, 191
Office manager, 53
Operations research analyst, 167
Operator, computer, 77
Opthalmologist, 173
Optometrist, 193
Oral pathologist, 81
Oral surgeon, 81
Orchard grower, 137
Orthodontist, 81
Orthopedic surgeon, 173
Orthotist, 171
Outdoor recreation director, 217

Paleomagnetician, 125
Paleontologist, 123, 125
Parasitologist, 177
Park naturalist, 243
Parole officer, 223
Patent drafter, 89
Patent lawyer, 157
Pathologist, 173
Pediatrician, 173
Penologist, 225
Performance specialist, 235
Performer, 79, 181
Periodontist, 81
Personnel manager, 55, 165, 211

The Career Connection for College Education

Petroleum engineer, 59
Petroleum geologist, 123
Petroleum geologist engineer, 123
Petrologist, 123
Pharmaceutical salesperson, 171
Pharmacist, 195
Photograph retoucher, 71
Photographer, 71, 73, 239
Photography director, TV, 73
Photojournalist, 73
Physical education teacher, 199
Physical facilities planner, 141
Physical geographer, 121, 191
Physical metallurgist, 175
Physical oceanographer, 191
Physical or social anthropologist, 43
Physical plant administrator/super-
    visor, 141
Physical therapist, 201
Physicist, 203
Physiologist, animal, 243
Physiologist, exercise, 199
Piano technician, 181
Placement director, 55
Planning/cartographic technician,
    121
Plant breeder, 51, 137
Plant cytologist, 51
Plant engineer, 141
Plant manager, 169
Plant pathologist, 51, 137
Plasma physicist, 203
Playwright, 235
Poet, 103
Political scientist, 205
Pollution control officer, 105
Poultry manager, 41
Poultry scientist, 41
Power/solid-state engineer, 97
Preschool teacher, 91
Principal, 101, 221
Probate lawyer, 157
Probation officer, 209, 223
Probation/parole officer, 209
Process control programmer, 77

Proctologist, 173
Production chemist, 61
Professional, boy scout, 217, 241
Professor, numerous
Project engineer, 163
Promotion manager, 29, 213
Proofreader, 103
Property accountant, 27
Prose writer, 103
Prosthetist, 171
Prosthodontist, 81
Psychiatric social worker, 223
Psychiatrist, 173
Psychologist
    clinical, 209
    counseling, 95, 209
    experimental, 209
    industrial, 209
    school, 95, 209
    social, 209
    sports, 131, 199, 209
Psychometrician, 167
Public health administrator, 75
Public health educator, 131
Public health nurse, 185
Public health nutritionist, 87, 185
Public health officer, 105, 113
Public health scientist, 177
Public health worker, 105
Public librarian, 159
Public relations specialist, 33, 39,
    49, 57, 63, 73, 107, 117, 127, 149,
    155, 183, 207, 219, 227
Public relations staff, 213
Public services director, 211
Publications editor, 33, 39, 49, 57,
    103, 107, 155, 183
Purchasing agent, 55, 165, 211

Quality control engineer, 163
Quality control lab technician, 177
Quality control officer, 105, 113
Quality controller, 233
Quick sketch artist, 47

Radio newscaster, 151
Radio/TV announcer, 73
Radiological technologist, 171
Radiologist, 173
Range manager, 37, 215
Real estate lawyer, 157
Receptionist, 145
Recreation director, 199, 217
Recreation supervisor, 217
Recreational therapist, 209, 217
Reference librarian, 159
Registered Nurse, 185
Remedial teacher, 221
Reporter, 151
Research and development officer, numerous
Research assistant, numerous
Research chemist, 61
Research dietitian, 87
Research engineer, 97
Research engineer, aeronautical, 31
Research horticulturist, 137
Research trainee, numerous
Researcher, numerous
Resource teacher, 95
Respiratory therapist, 171
Retail manager, 55, 165
Revenue agent, 27
Rural bank manager, 35
Rural sociologist, 225

Safety manager, 187, 211
Sales agent, 147
Sales manager, 55, 165
Sales representative, 29, 37, 69
Salesperson, numerous
Sanitarian, 131
Sanitation engineer, 65
Sanitation officer, 105
School counselor, 95
School librarian, 159
School psychologist, 95, 209
School secretary, 145
School social worker, 223
Science writer, 61

Scientific linguist, 63, 67, 117, 127, 149, 161, 207, 219, 227
Scientific programmer, 77
Scientific writer, 63, 117, 127, 149, 207, 219, 227
Scientist, numerous
Scout executive, See Boy Scout Professional
Screenwriter, 103
Sculptor, 47
Secretary, numerous
Securities trader, 27
Seismologist, 123, 125
Senior and executive vice-president, 111
Set designer, 47
Set illustrator, 71
Social caseworker, 223, 225
Social ecologist, 225
Social group worker, 223
Social pathologist, 225
Social psychologist, 209
Social service assistant, 223
Social worker, certified, 223
Social worker, fellow, 223
Social worker, graduate (MSW), 223
Social worker, medical, 223
Social worker, psychiatric, 223
Social worker, school, 223
Sociologist, 225
Soil conservationist, 137
Soil scientist, 37, 61
Soil/water conservationist, 37
Solid-state physicist, 203
Special collections librarian, 159
Special education teacher, 95
Speech pathologist, 231
Sports director, intramural, 199
Sports psychologist, 131, 199, 209
State rehabilitation counselor, 95
Statistician, 167, 233
Stenographer, 145
Stockbroker, 55, 93
Story editor, 103
Stratigrapher, 123, 125

Stress analyst, aeronautical, 31
Structural drafter, 89
Structural engineer, 65
Studio artist, 47
Substance abuse counselor, 95
Supervisor, numerous
Supervisor of historic sites, 133
Supervisor of word processing, 145
Surgeon, 173
Systems analyst, 55, 77, 211, 233
Systems engineer, 97
Systems programmer, 77, 85

Tax accountant, 27
Tax attorney, 157
Tax specialist, 27
Teacher, numerous
Technical director, 235
Technical illustrator, 71
Technical scientific editor, 103
Technical teacher, 143
Technical writer, 103, 131
Technician
    archaeological, 43
    chemical engineer, 59
    chemical lab, 61
    civil engineer, 65
    dialysis, 171
    electrical power, 99
    electrocardiographic, 171
    electroencepholographic, 171
    electronics, 99
    engineering, 89
    forestry, 115, 239
    industrial engineer, 85
    industrial laboratory, 163
    library, 159
    materials science, 163
    medical lab, 171
    metallurgical engineering, 175
    metals/materials, 175
    mining engineer, 179
    museum, 43
    piano, 181
    planning/cartographic, 121

quality control lab, 177
Technologist
    agribusiness, 35
    chemical, 61
    civil engineering, 65
    communications, 99
    computer, 99
    cytotechnologist, 171
    dairy, 41
    food, 105, 113
    medical, 171
    microbiology, 177
    nuclear medical, 171
    radiological, 171
    tissue, 171
    ultrasound, 171
    X-ray, 171
Television and audio systems
    specialist, 99
TV announcer, 73
TV director, 73, 235
TV news broadcaster, 151
Terminal operator, 145
Test engineer, aeronautical, 31
Test kitchen specialist, 113
Textile converter, 69
Theater costume designer, 69
Theoretical mathematician, 167
Theoretical physicist, 203
Therapist
    art, 47
    blind, for the, 95
    industrial, 209
    manual arts, 143, 209
    music, 181
    occupational, 189
    physical, 201
    recreational, 209, 217
    respiratory, 171
Tissue technologist, 171
Title attorney, 157
Tool design drafter, 89
Tool designer, 163
Tool programmer, 163
Topographical drafter, 89

Training director, 241
Transcribing machine operator, 145
Translator, 63, 67, 117, 127, 149,
161, 207, 219, 227
Transportation director, 55, 211
Transportation engineer, 65
Travel agent, 33, 39, 49, 57, 63, 107,
117, 121, 127, 149, 155, 183, 207,
219, 227
Treasurer, 111
Trust officer, 111
Typist, 145

Ultrasound technologist, 171
Underwriter, 111
University relations, 213
Urban planner, 45
Urban region planner, 121
Urban sociologist, 225
Urologist, 173

Veterinarian, 237
Veterinary anatomist, 237
Veterinary bacteriologist, 237
Veterinary epidemiologist, 237
Veterinary pathologist, 237
Veterinary physiologist, 237
Veterinary virologist, 237
Vocational educator, 143, 215

Welfare officer, 223
Wildlife biologist, 239, 243
Wildlife manager, 239, 243
Word processing supervisor, 145
Writer
    copywriter, 73, 103
    correspondent, 33, 39, 49, 57,
        107, 151, 155, 183, 205
    editorial, 137, 197
    journalist, 73, 151
    playwright, 235
    poetry, 103
    prose, 103
    scientific, 63, 117, 121, 149, 207,
        219, 227
    technical, 103, 131

Writer, researcher, 203

X-ray technologist, 171

Youth agency administrator, 241

Zoologist, 243

OCCUPATIONAL OUTLOOK HANDBOOK
1994-1995 Edition — *By U.S. Department of Labor*

This low-cost JIST edition of the U.S. Department of labor's popular career exploration guide describes the 250 jobs in which 85% of the American workforce is employed. Valuable information about each occupation includes a description of the work itself, employment outlook and opportunities, earnings, related occupations, training and advancement, and sources of additional information.

OTHER INFORMATION
- THE standard career reference book
- The most widely used and known career reference for professionals and schools
- Includes the latest Department of Labor statistics

8-1/2 x 11, Paper, 473 pp. ISBN 1-56370-160-X **$15.95** *Order Code OOH4*	8-1/2 x 11, Hardback, 473 pp. ISBN 1-56370-161-8 **$21.95** *Order Code OOHH4*

AMERICA'S TOP JOBS MULTIMEDIA
A Multimedia Computer Program Providing Information on Over 250 Jobs

This computer software integrates text, sound, voice, and still full-color images featuring information found in the *Occupational Outlook Handbook*. Careful attention has been given to make this software easy to use--so easy, we think that it is even fun! Search for occupations in a number of ways including earnings, educational requirements, and employment.

ISBN 1-56370-113-8 **3 1/2 Disk** *Order Code ATJM3* **$295.00**	ISBN 1-56370-115-4 **5 1/4 Disk** *Order Code ATJM5* **$295.00**	ISBN 1-56370-167-7 **CD Rom** *Order Code ATJMCD* **$295.00**

*Look for these and other fine books from **JIST Works, Inc.**, at your full service bookstore or call us for additional information at 800-648-5478.*

DICTIONARY OF OCCUPATIONAL TITLES

Revised Fourth Edition

This is THE definitive career reference book compiled by the U.S. Department of Labor. The DOT's classification system is THE standard for describing jobs. Each job code reveals the level of skills required to work with people, data, and things, and each job description includes detailed occupational information. It's organized by major job categories and cross-referenced by industry and job title.

ISBN 1-56370-006-9	ISBN 1-56370-000-X
Hardback 1 Vol.	**Paper 2 Vol.**
Order Code: DOTH	*Order Code: DOT91*
$48.00	**$39.00**

THE COMPLETE GUIDE FOR OCCUPATIONAL EXPLORATION — *By JIST Editorial Staff*

First revision since 1984! Based on the new *Dictionary of Occupational Titles, The Complete Guide* contains up-to-date information on today's occupations, many of which have been created or greatly changed by technology. More than 12,000 occupations are organized into:

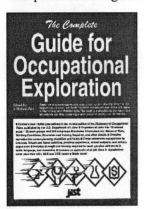

- 12 major interests areas
- 66 work groups
- 348 subgroups of related jobs

Includes an alphabetical appendix listing almost 30,000 jobs.

OTHER INFORMATION

- A must book for career counselors, professionals, and school personnel
- The only book of its kind with up-to-date information
- One of the three major reference books used by job placement counselors

8-1/2 x 11, Paper, 936 pp.	8-1/2 x 11, Hardback, 936 pp.
ISBN 1-56370-052-2	ISBN 1-56370-100-6
Order Code CGOE	*Order Code CGOEH*
$34.95	**$44.95**

*Look for these and other fine books from **JIST Works, Inc.**, at your full service bookstore or call us for additional information at 800-648-5478.*

HIRE LEARNING—Your Guide to a Successful School-to-Work
Transition — *Newly Revised! A Complete Three-Book Curriculum!*
Developed by Patricia Duffy and Walter Wannie

This is a complete and major revision of the widely acclaimed curriculum. *Hire Learning* has been field tested with thousands of students and reinforces the importance of basic academic skills and responsible behavior to prepare students for a successful transition from school to work. The three-book set includes both interesting text and activities—everything needed to present the material in a class or individual setting.
Instructor's Guide also available.

Setting Your Career and Life Direction	Landing a Job	Succeeding in Your Work and Community
ISBN 1-56370-188-X	ISBN 1-56370-189-8	ISBN 1-56370-190-1
8-1/2 x 11, Paper, 112 pp.	8-1/2 x 11, Paper, 112 pp.	8-1/2 x 11, Paper, 112 pp.
Order Code J188X	*Order Code J1898*	*Order Code J1901*
$8.95	**$8.95**	**$8.95**

GETTING THE JOB YOU REALLY WANT 2nd Edition
A Step-by-Step Guide
by J. Michael Farr

This intensive career planning and job search workbook helps readers clarify what they want in a job and provides specific information on more than 200 careers. Those who know what kind of job they want will find help in identifying the skills to emphasize in interviews and information on relationed jobs.

OTHER INFORMATION:

- Easy to read and use
- Includes activities, examples, and checklists
- Techniques to cut job search time in half

8-1/2 x 11, Paper, 148 pp.
ISBN 1-56370-092-1
Order Code RWR
$9.95

*Look for these and other fine books from **JIST Works, Inc.**, at your full service bookstore or call us for additional information at 800-648-5478.*

AMERICA'S TOP JOBS FOR COLLEGE GRADUATES
Detailed Information on Jobs and Trends for College Grads — and Those Considering a College Education
by U.S. Department of Labor and J. Michael Farr

Nearly 2 million graduates enter or reenter the job market each year. This newest addition to JIST's America's series explains why college graduates can expect to make more money and defines the latest labor market and career planning trends through the year 2005. Also includes information on the 500 most popular jobs, and details on employment trends by major industry.

OTHER INFORMATION:

- Comprehensive appendices
- Based on the most current information from the Department of Labor
- Special section on job search and career planning

8-1/2 x 11, Paper, 300 pp.
ISBN 1-56370-140-5
Order Code ATCG
$14.95

AMERICA'S TOP TECHNICAL AND TRADE JOBS
Good Jobs That Don's Require Four Years of College
Edited and Compiled by J. Michael Farr

Like the other books in this series, this book provides job descriptions for more than 50 of the top technical and trade jobs in the U.S. economy. As many as 80 percent of the new jobs created do not require a college degree but do require technical skills! Determine which skills to upgrade to remain competitive in the work force and move up in your career.

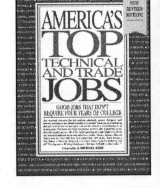

OTHER INFORMATION:

- Over 50 detailed job descriptions
- Other solid data on 300 jobs
- Special section on job search and career planning

8-1/2 x 11, Paper, 232 pp.
ISBN 1-56370-116-2
Order Code ATT
$11.95

---

*Look for these and other fine books from **JIST Works, Inc.**, at your full service bookstore or call us for additional information at 800-648-5478.*

THE QUICK RESUME and COVER LETTER BOOK —
Write and Use an Effective Resume in Only One Day
By J. Michael Farr

First title in JIST's new Quick Guides series, by a best-selling author whose job search books have sold more than one million copies! Contains an "Instant Resume Worksheet" that enables job seekers to put together a basic, acceptable resume in less than one day. Provides helpful advice on creating job objectives, identifying skills, dealing with special situations, and getting a job.

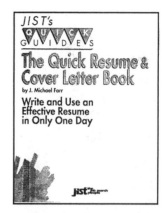

OTHER INFORMATION:

- Logical structure makes information easy to locate
- Contains more than 50 sample resumes and cover letters
- Crucial career planning and job search sections

7 x 9, Paper, 288 pp.
ISBN 1-56370-141-3
Order Code RCLQG
$9.95

JOB SAVVY — *How To Be a Success at Work*
by LaVerne Ludden Ed.D.

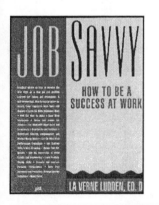

This book was written to help new employees learn the basics of successful job behavior such as good attendance, punctuality, and reliability. Job Savvy focuses on developing workplace skills that pay off—skills that get results that can get you noticed. Too many people learn the hard way about what it takes to get ahead on a job. Get a jump start on your successful career after reading this book!

OTHER INFORMATION:

- Separate Instructor's Guide
- Many exercises, forms, and worksheets
- Thorough, practical advice

8-1/2 x 11, Paper, 169 pp.
ISBN 0-942784-79-0
Order Code JS
$10.95

---

*Look for these and other fine books from **JIST Works, Inc.**, at your full service bookstore or call us for additional information at 800-648-5478.*